CU00641928

ALL MUCK AND NETTLES

Cover photographs
Burling and Mending (Bradford Heritage Recording Unit)
The Author aged eighteen (Author's collection)

ALL MUCK AND NETTLES!
The Early Life of Burler and Mender No.57

by
Vera Smith

BRADFORD LIBRARIES AND INFORMATION SERVICE

Published by Bradford Libraries and Information Service 1990
Central Library,
Prince's Way,
Bradford,
West Yorkshire
BD1 1NN

Typeset by Ryburn Typesetting Ltd, Halifax
Printed by The Amadeus Press Ltd, Huddersfield

British Library Cataloguing in Publication Data
Smith, Vera
  All muck and nettles: the early life of Burler and Mender
  no. 57.
  1. West Yorkshire (England). Social life, history. 1918–
  1945
  I. Title II. Bradford Libraries and Information Service
  942.817083

ISBN 0-907734-23-5

Dedication

This short history of my young days is dedicated
to the memory of my mother

Annie Brook Magson

– a wonderful mother and my best friend.

Contents

Illustrations

Preface

When Vera Smith told me, with some pride, of the rich and varied life she had had, and of the many mills in which she had worked, I suggested she should write it all down. I thought no more of the incident. I was, therefore, greatly surprised when she triumphantly dropped 106 pages of typescript on my desk a few short months later. Naturally I was pleased that she had responded so positively to my suggestion. But being busy at the time, I passed Vera's work to some of my colleagues. Their enthusiasm made me read it myself, and what I read excited me as well. Clearly here was a story teller of great talent and a story of great interest. A life of some poverty in those hard years between the wars is described in such vivid detail that the reader is swept along totally absorbed in Vera's homes, her play, her school, her work, her feelings and hopes. Here is a world of mean housing and household drudgery, long hours and tyrannical supervisors, hunger and tragedy. But here also are school days that *were* happy, of people who *were* kind, and of people who *did* enjoy themselves. Above all, here is a girl growing to womanhood, sensitive and thoughtful, who looked for the good in people. Despite the clouds, the sun is always there. I now feel far richer for the experience, and more than a little humbled – those really were hard times. Thank you Vera, for giving us the opportunity to share your experiences.

It but remains for my colleagues and myself to commend your memories to others in the hope that they, too, will be enriched.

Bob Duckett
Senior Librarian, Reference Services
Bradford Libraries and Information Service

Editorial Note

In order to protect the guilty, "Miss Tailor" is a pseudonym.

Acknowledgements

My thanks to the many people who helped in the writing of this book –
Bob Duckett who suggested I write it.

My husband Leslie Smith for support and encouragement.

My brother Donald Magson for family photos.

Sheila Rix for her excellence in reading my writing and for typing
the script.

Pudsey Civic Society for help with old pictures.

The staff of Bradford Libraries and Information Service for all
their help.

Mr and Mrs John Calvert of Pudsey for the reproduction of
pictures of Pudsey.

Bradford Heritage Recording Unit, Bradford Libraries and
Information Service, and the *Telegraph & Argus* for photographs.

CHAPTER 1

"Muck or nettles" as they say. First things ...

I was born on the 8th September 1922 at 67 Wilberforce Street Laisterdyke in the parish of St Mary's, Bradford. My mother wanted me named Dorothy Mavis but when Dad got to the Registry Office he changed his mind and called me Vera.

My parents were James William Magson and Annie Brook. Just a brief word about them both. My father was the eldest child of Alfred and Alice Magson who lived at 67 Wilberforce Street, Sticker Lane, Laisterdyke, in the city of Bradford. My mother's parents were Sam and Sarah Brook of 88 Valley Road, Pudsey – all the Brook family were from Pudsey.

My grandad Magson was a remarkable man in more ways than one. He was very tall, six foot, with dark curly hair, very strong build with a fresh complexion. He was a blacksmith on the railway and worked at the Adolphus Street Sheds down Wakefield Road. Before I was born a flying piece of steel had entered his eye so he only had one eye, the other was just a hollow. Nevertheless he was the most jolly man I have ever known. He was the life and soul of any company he was in. He drank like a fish, loved his beer, the more he drank the merrier he became. I can see him now, ready for work – a flat cap on his curly head, a thick union shirt with a red kerchief round his neck, an old jacket and thick moleskin trousers. His dinner all tied up in a red handkerchief he carried in his hand. On Sundays he wore his lovely navy blue serge suit with a stiff collar to his shirt; a waistcoat, and across the waistcoat, a thick gold chain with a gold pocket watch in one side and a gold drop in the middle; a smart "Billy Cock" bowler hat on his head and grey spats over his shoes. He looked lovely, my grandad, and I loved him very much. He was never too busy to take me on his knee in the big wooden chair (we call them Windsor chairs now) and tell me about 'Red Riding Hood and the Wolf' or 'Goldilocks and the Three Bears'. The stories he told were never read out of a book but told in his own words with all the sound effects put in, like a deep growling voice for the wolf, and different voices for the three bears. I used to sit on his knee and shiver in anticipation of the delights to come, he made every

"I was born at 67 Wilberforce Street, Laisterdyke." Wilberforce Street, 1961.
Photo: Bradford Libraries and Information Services

story one of wonder and delight. He would have made a fortune these days on television.

My grandma Magson was a different kettle of fish altogether. She was small with fair hair and complexion and my father, myself and my two brothers all took after her. Not in being small, indeed we are all very tall, I am 5ft 8in, both my brothers, Donald and Basil, are over 6ft but we all have blonde hair, blue eyes and very fair skin. Anyhow, to get back to Gran. She was in complete command of the house and everyone in it. You did what she said and did it at once, or, you got smacked. You never ever gave cheek or answered back; her word was the law at No.67. She was the person in the street who they all came to for help, no matter what the circumstances. She laid out the people who died and the babies born in Wilberforce Street had her there to guide them into the world. In those days women did not go to hospital to have babies, they were born at home. Not many had midwives – they could not afford it – so ladies like Gran were called upon all the time. Many times I remember being snug in bed at Gran's when a voice was heard shouting outside the bedroom window – "Can you come Alice, 'baby' is coming" –

14

and she got up, put on her clothes and was not seen again until a new baby was safely delivered. Also she knew a lot about cures for all ailments. You were given treacle and sulphur for spots and heat lumps and a 'good clear out'. Goose grease rubbed in great dollops all over your chest and back for chest colds. For a sore throat, a sweaty stocking tied round your neck to go to bed, and if that did not work, horror upon horror, you were given the dreadful cure of a teaspoon of sugar with Friar's Balsam on it. This was horrible to swallow and made me really feel sick, but it was no use crying, it was tipped down your throat and you made the best of it. Funny, even now in these days this is the remedy that never fails for me if I have a sore throat. Next was 'Dicky Orange' for cuts, septic fingers or any sores that would not heal. A thick slice like a square piece of licorice but with a canvas coating round it. She lit a taper and held it to the end of the Dicky Orange and as the black stuff melted it fell on the septic sore. This was then wrapped in a cotton bandage and kept on until all the pus was drawn out. Mustard plasters were another favourite, spread on brown paper. These were very embarrassing for when you moved the paper rustled and everyone knew what you were wearing. She used a lot of herbs as well. Camomile for tea, dreaded senna pods to make you fly like hell to the toilet and Monastery Herbs for stomach upsets. Peppermint tea for all wind (north, south, east, west) and anything else anyone could think of, also comfrey for sprains and pains.

They were two entirely different people, each in their own way indispensable to the people they lived among.

My grandparents on my mother's side I never knew, never even saw a picture of them. Samuel Brook and his wife Sarah both died before I was born, my mother very rarely spoke about them. He was a boot and shoe maker, not a cobbler, and had his own little business. Grandma Brook just produced children. Five girls – Ethel, Martha, Janey, Fanny and Annie. Four boys – Arthur, James, Harry and Percy. So nine children, of which six were married but my mother was the only one in the entire family to have children. My two brothers and I are the only line back to the Brook family of Pudsey. Three of the family, Martha, Fanny and Percy, never got married. That is a brief summary of my mother's and father's background.

My dad joined the army in 1917 at the age of 18 years. He was wounded in the trenches and was sent home for convalescence and leave, he never went back as he was discharged. He met Mum, they became engaged and married in 1921. Before the war he was a clerk in a wool

"Grandad managed to get Dad a job at the Adolphus Street Works."
Photo: John Marshall

warehouse in Bradford. After the war, like thousands more, he had no job to return to. This made him very bitter and during the whole of his life he never ever spoke about his war days, he said it was something he wanted to forget. However, he never forgot that the country he fought for rewarded him with no job, no home and no prospects. It made him turn to the Labour Party and he did become a trade union member and, after a lot of years, a union officer for the National Union of Railways. This happened because Grandad was, as I said before, a blacksmith on the railways and he, after a while, managed to get Dad a job at the Adolphus Street Works as a labourer. He worked on the steam engines; very dirty, hard work, for which he was paid the marvellous sum of 32/-. Thirty two shillings per week to eventually keep and feed five people.

My mother was a weaver in the mills, and when she and Dad were married she came over to Laisterdyke to live with Dad's family at 67 Wilberforce Street. She went to work at Priestley's Mills up Sticker Lane. Wilberforce Street was a long row of back to back cottages that stretched from Sticker Lane right up nearly to Byronstone Road.

16

The houses are no longer there these days, but Westbury Street is still there which crosses from Parsonage Road over to Broad Lane and this road cut Wilberforce Street in half. No.67 was on the left hand side in the top half. The houses were in groups of four in front and four at the back with a long passage between the fours. All the houses were the same, one large living room with one window, a cooking range with oven at one side and a hot water boiler at the other, the fire itself and a large shelf along the top. There was no kitchen, just a cellar head with no window. The sink was stone with one cold water tap. There was just enough room for the great big mangle for the washing with a zinc tub on the top of it, then you were down the steps into the cellar. The coal was kept in one half, and in the other there were two long stone shelves where food was kept, which had to be covered up well because the cellar was so damp snails were all over the place. When I was older and visited Gran and Grandad I hated going down there. All over the walls were silver marks where the snails had crawled. Gran used to take a shovel and some salt down, and I have seen her come up with 10 or 14 snails on the shovel which she then threw on the fire. There was one large bedroom with two double beds. Gran and Grandad in one, Auntie Mary and Auntie Hetty in the other and there they had to sleep until they both got married – there was no privacy in those days. Up some more stairs was a small attic with one skylight window, very dark it was, and in there were two single beds for Dad and Uncle Albert. To reach the outside toilet you came out of the front door, walked past two houses through the dark passage to a toilet that was shared by another family. It was dreadful on a cold dark night to get there and find it occupied, as it meant waiting in the cold before you got in. It was awful as well if the candle you had taken for a bit of light blew out and you had no match to relight it. It was awful as well if Gran had been dosing you with sulphur and treacle and you had the runs.

This then was the situation when Mum and Dad got married and came to live at 67. They had to go across the street and sleep in a neighbour's attic for 4/- per week. Mother hated it (she told me years later) but houses were like jobs (very hard to get) so it was muck or nettles as they say. When she found out she was pregnant, things were worse than ever. Anyhow, after I was born things were really desperate. Seven adults and a baby in a tiny cottage, all cooking to be done on an open fire, no cookers in those days. All hot water had to be ladled out of the fire boiler, it must have been terrible, one sink for seven adults to try and get washed in the morning before going to work.

When I was six months old they got a house, Mum says she cried with joy about it. The house was at Pudsey, about 300 yards from her own family home where Auntie Martha, Auntie Fanny, Uncle Jim and Uncle Harry all still lived as they were all yet unmarried. Auntie Martha had asked the landlady who had a lot of houses around Valley Road for an empty cottage at No.8 Valley Road. So off Mum and Dad went with me in a basket to settle in. A horse and cart brought one or two bits of furniture for them. Most of the furniture had been given by Auntie Martha, her house being a large family house and a few having left on getting married, she had beds and chairs left over and very kindly gave them to Mum.

So in the year 1923 my life began at No.8 Valley Road and very happy we all were, Mum, Dad and me. The house was a stone built cottage in a row of six, there was a nice area of grass in front of the cottages, and then the back windows of another row of six which were a bit larger than ours at the front. At the end of the row there was a wall built and the toilets were at the end, three toilets, dry ones, for six houses. Also next to them there was a stone building with a flat stone roof with a large round hole in it. At the front there were two strong wooden doors, the top one opened and in there we put all the ashes from the fires in the houses and all household waste, things like cans or potato peelings or anything that could not be burnt on the coal fires. This stone building was a favourite place for all the children to play when we got older. We used to climb up the doors on to the flat top near the hole and sit around and tell stories or play games. You see the roof was always lovely and warm because all the red hot ashes from the fires, from both rows of houses went in there. The hole was to let out the smoke and we always knew in winter when the roof was warm enough to sit on due to the smoke pouring out. Every two weeks during the night when everybody was in bed, the night soil men came round to empty them. They had horses and carts and shovels, they would open the bottom doors and throw out everything that had been in there burning for two weeks.

There was a small pavement in front of the houses and we played hopscotch and skipped on the pavement, we also played with our bouncy balls. Those were very, very happy days, no money, not many clothes, entertainment nil, no pictures, no television – it was not thought of then! We had a piano and my Dad played a bit but there were no wireless sets in those days.

CHAPTER 2

"Nine years of happiness". School days

At the age of five I was taken to Littlemoor Council School, Valley Road, to start my school days. The school is still there and whenever I go past I look at it with love, full of overwhelming memories of the nine years of happiness at that school. In my day, you spent all your time at the one school, going from infants to junior and then senior before you finished. I was lucky in more ways than one. The school was 100 yards from our house so there was no long walk on cold winter mornings for me, just a quick sprint to get into the playground before the bell went. Right from the beginning I took to it like a 'duck to water', everything I did there I enjoyed, so the saying 'the happiest days of your life' was a true one for me.

Our headmistress in the infants was Miss Ward. I can see her now, tall and thin with glasses, her greying hair pulled on top of her head in a bun. A long black skirt reaching the ground, black button boots and always a white blouse with a high stiff collar like the men wore, with two little pieces of celluloid on either side of the opening at the front to keep the collar stiff and straight. Owing to this, she could not easily bend her head down so she sort of looked down her nose at you when speaking.

At morning assembly we all stood in rows facing her desk in the hall, and sang a short hymn – "Jesus bids us shine with a pure clear light, Like a little candle burning in the night" – this was a great favourite. Then hands together, eyes closed while we all said "Our Father, Who art in heaven". While we said our prayers with closed eyes, Miss Ward walked in front of each line of boys and girls, from the front to the back of the hall. As she did this, she inspected our shoes or boots, our faces to see if clean and hair to see if combed and tidy. If you had dirty shoes, dirty face or untidy hair you got a sharp smack on your bottom from the short cane she carried in her hand. This had a great effect on any new pupils, after one or two smacks you made sure you were clean and tidy for Miss Ward. On looking round at some of the pupils in our schools today I think a few Miss Wards would be a great improvement. We all learned our ABC and could say the alphabet right through, we also learned to count. This was done in a most unusual way. Never having gone to any other school but Littlemoor, I do not know if this method was standard. On our small slates (yes, we had slates and slate pencils) we were each given about 20 very tiny cowrie shells; they have a lovely pale yellow colour with brown inside. We all loved playing with those little shells, but in playing we were also learning. The teacher would say "Take four of your shells and put them on the other side of your slate", so we all moved 4 tiny shells across from one side to the other. When we were all finished she would say, "Now move another 7 shells", again a great deal of counting and pushing of shells across the slate. "Now children, count how many shells you have taken from the first pile". "Eleven shells teacher", we all called out. "So how many are left in the first pile", more counting. "Nine shells left Miss", we all said. So $4 + 7 = 11$ and 11 from 20 leaves 9, and so it was. To divide we were told to put the same number of shells in each corner of the slate and we found that 4 small piles of 5 shells made 20. None of the children in my class went into junior school without being able to spell small words, like dog, cat, hat, mat, bat and we could all do small sums of addition and subtraction and division.

On reaching junior school we were put into small groups of five or six, all with our reading books and we all read a full chapter aloud to the children in our group. If you faltered over one word there was always someone who knew it and put you right. As we became more fluent we started at the top of the class and everyone stood up in turn and read a sentence. Likewise with our tables. We started with 2 x 1 are 2, then 2 x 2 are 4, right up to 2 x 12 are 24. The tables were said like poems, recited every morning without fail and even now, nearly 70 years on, I can still remember all the times tables.

The headmaster over both junior and senior at Littlemoor was a gentleman called Mr. Harold Threapleton, I remember him to this day. A very tall straight man, held himself like a soldier and walked like one. Always wore a beautiful black jacket and grey pinstripe trousers. Always a white shirt, black, highly polished shoes and always a bowler hat on his head. His word was law and no-one spoke back, looked away or lied when confronted with our respected headmaster. He demanded respect, complete obedience and absolute truthfulness from everyone (and he got it). Even out of school, Saturday or Sunday, if you chanced to meet him outside it was "Good morning, Sir" or "Good afternoon, Sir", and there was no hiding behind a lamp post or your parents. The boys had

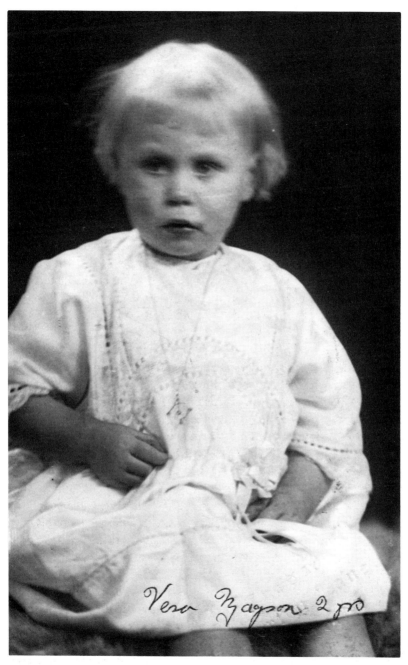

Vera Magson aged two years. *Photo: Author's collection*

to take off their caps when addressing him, all the boys at school in those days had to wear school caps. If you were caught talking in the classroom, or any other misconduct, the teacher would say "Go stand outside the class door" and once you were out there you were stood in the hall where Mr Threapleton had his desk. When he saw you stood outside the classroom he just beckoned with one finger for you to approach his desk. When stood there in fear and trembling, you were asked your offence, and it was indeed a terrible moment, one that I tried very hard not to have to go through. Most offences were dealt with by a very stern talk, but if you offended more than twice in one week, then it was the cane on one hand. He had only to talk very sternly to me and I dissolved into tears. You see, I loved and respected him very much and it upset me to have him angry with me. Sometimes he would say, "I am very disappointed with you Vera, I expect better behaviour from you". This made me feel worse than ever, to think he was disappointed with me so I would then try even harder to gain his praise. This man had a great influence over my young life. I looked up to him, wanted to please him and tried very hard in all things to do better in my school work.

I was very fond of, and indeed excelled in three subjects all my years at school. I was always near the top in written English, History and Geography. The teacher who taught us History was called Mr Donald Stock, and thanks to him I found a love of history of this country which I have kept all through the years. I still get history books from the library even now, some of which I have read over and over. I can still name every King and Queen of England since Harold at the Battle of Hastings, to our own Elizabeth. In most cases I know the names of their wives or husbands and their children. The important battles, both at sea and on land, the victories and defeats, the heroes and traitors. What a marvellous country is our England, and the people who have helped to make her.

Every Empire Day, which used to be the 24th May, all the school had to gather in the big hall. There we stood, every class, from the seniors at the back all in straight rows, down to the juniors at the front, all facing Mr Threapleton at his desk. The piano would start playing and everyone stood to attention to sing this hymn. I always remember the words and the tune as well:

What heroes thou has bred, oh England my Country
I see the mighty dead pass in line
Each with undaunted heart, playing his gallant part

22

Littlemoor Council School today. *Photo: Author's collection*

making thee what thou art
England of mine.

Our Fathers loved thee well, oh England my Country
for thee they fought and fell over the brine
Ready to hear thy call, ready to fight and fall
ready to give thee all
England of mine.

Then let me take my place, oh England my Country
Amid the gallant race that is thine
Ready to hear thy call, ready to fight and fall
ready to give thee all
England of mine.

How patriotic we felt in those days, the Union Jack, our King George and Queen Mary, our victory in the terrible 1914–18 war, all the young men who had died, that we could stand there on Empire Day in the 1930's and be proud of them, and our Country and Empire. After singing the hymn we all stood still and said aloud:

23

I will remember that I am a member of a great brotherhood
And I will endeavour to leave my Country greater and not less
Than it was entrusted to me

That was our Empire Day Pledge.

One day when I was in the top form (sixth form), the headmaster came into the class. In his hand was a composition book and he looked very pleased, so we all knew there would be nothing we had done to upset or displease him. He asked our teacher, Mrs Middlebrook, if he could just read aloud an essay with which he was very impressed. He told us it was from one of the sixth formers, so we were all very much interested. He had only spoken about five words when I realised that the essay was mine. I felt myself getting hot and red around the face, as he went on reading. On finishing he said it was one of the best English essays he had read for a long, long time and he had marked it excellent. Then he said "Thank you Vera for such a wonderful effort". At playtime all my friends said how good it had been to listen to. I told my parents and they too were very pleased with me.

My mother had a lovely singing voice, a clear true soprano. She had been in the choir at our chapel. I was indeed proud to have inherited this gift from her and have been singing all my life. At home, in concerts when young, in pantomimes and in various church choirs during my years. At school I was often called out of the classroom and into the hall where the piano was, the music class was always held in the hall. Many times I have been asked to sing school songs in front of the different classes gathered there. This I enjoyed, singing was something I really enjoyed and it held no fears for me.

CHAPTER 3

"If you were lucky ... a bit of linoleum."
Homes and houses

While my school life went on, over the years things happened at home. When I was six my brother Donald was born. I knew I was getting a little brother or sister because Mum had told me. I was really looking forward to it but one thing did bother me. Some people, including one or two aunties, kept saying that when the new arrival came I would 'get my nose pushed out'. I did not know if this was going to hurt me or not, I did not like to ask who was going to 'push it out' but I had the idea it was going to be the new baby. So when he arrived I viewed him a bit warily at first until I realised no way could he do anything to my nose, he was much too small. I have often thought it was a silly thing to say to a small child and have never used that saying to any child, knowing how upset I felt. Donald was a lovely baby, very good with a lovely head of silver, blonde hair, blue eyes and a pink and white complexion. As he grew older he got tall for his age like me, but his hair never changed from the lovely silver blonde. I could pick him out even in a playground full of other children. Now at the age of sixty his hair is blonde but any silver these days is through age.

Having another child meant we were over-crowded in our small house as there was only one bedroom. Mum asked our landlady, Mrs Glover, if she had another vacant house to let. As it happened a family living in the row in front of ours were moving out. They had six children and the house had only two bedrooms so they had got a house with three bedrooms. So we again moved house from the back row to the front, to No.18 Valley Road.

We were all absolutely thrilled with the new house. A large living room with the usual cooking range, which Mum polished till it looked like glass. There were two windows in the living room which made it nice and light. Talking about light, we had a gas light in the ceiling with three gas mantles, when you pulled the chains on the side of the fitment, then filled with gas, it was ready for lighting with either matches or a taper. They used to make quite a 'pop' when being lit. Dad bought a glass bowl to fit round the mantles and we thought it was wonderful and so modern. There was a cellar head kitchen with a long window and the dark brown sink was under this window, with the one cold water tap. Some long wood shelves for the pans and tins, then steps down into the cellar. We really had come up in the world because we also had a living kitchen as well. This was a long narrow room off from the cellar head and also had two windows and a small black iron fireplace, a set-pot boiler with a little door underneath it, which you opened and put in wood and paper to get it lit, then the coal and shut the door to get it going. On the top was a big round wood lid which lifted off, and when the set-pot was filled with cold water, the fire got it lovely and hot, so we had hot water for washing and everything else. Mum was delighted with this kitchen as when she did washing for other people she could put long lines of cord across it and dry the washing in there very quickly in winter when it was too cold to dry outside. The one drawback to this was on very cold days when we were cosy and warm in there we could not see each other for fog or steam from all the wet clothes. Mum had an old mangle to wring the clothes but the steam coming off them was something we had to live with. Having the kitchen with a fire in as well as the hot water from the set-pot meant we could have our Friday night baths in front of the fire, with loads of hot water. Dad would get the large zinc bath out of the cellar, put it in front of the fire and Mum filled it with hot water. The sheer luxury of those Friday night baths stays with me to this day. A clean nightie on and a hot cup of cocoa, all lovely and warm on a cold winter night was heaven. Before we went to bed, Dad filled the two stone hot water bottles (no rubber ones in those days) and put them in our beds. A candle in the holder was lit and the little procession went up the stone stairs to the back bedroom where two small beds were ready and waiting. Straight into bed and holding the bottle close, a good night kiss from Mum and Dad and a reminder to say our prayers and God Bless our family and home.

Funny how things continue from childhood. The houses were so cold in winter, no central heating, no carpets in bedrooms, if you were lucky perhaps a bit of linoleum down on the floor and a small tab Mum had made, at the side of the bed. So you did not play around but got into bed smart to keep warm. Even now I always say my prayers at night in bed. Some things change in our lives but this has never altered in mine.

So there we were in 1928 a nice little house, a nice family, no money but healthy and happy. I know for a fact that by Tuesday in the week

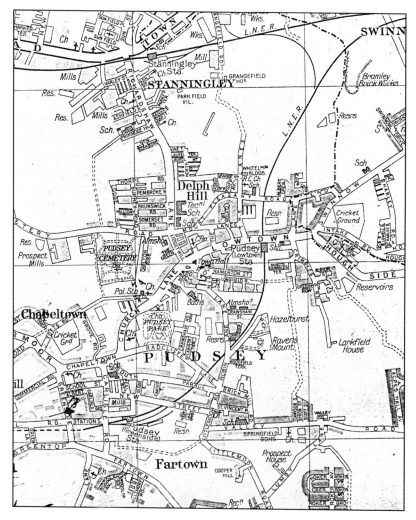

Map of Pudsey 1938.   *Courtesy Bradford Libraries and Information Service*

Mum was lucky to have 3d left in her purse to feed us with. Often she asked me to go down to Auntie Martha's (her eldest sister who lived in the family house) and ask her to lend Mum 1/- which she would pay back at the week end.

Auntie Martha and Auntie Fanny still lived in the old family house down Valley Road. Also there was Uncle Jim and Uncle Harry. Both sisters worked in the wool textile weavers at Cliff Mills at the top of

Valley Road, just across from where our house was. Cliff Mills have been derelict for years now, but recently on visiting Pudsey we went round there and a whole new estate of lovely houses, nearly all detached, have been built on the site and very nice they look, a big improvement. The Brook family house is there, down Valley Road, some day I am going to knock on the door to ask if, for memory's sake, would they let me just have a little look round, I hope they will. This house was the largest I have ever been in up until the age of about 9 or 10 years. You went up a steep flight of steps to the front door and there was a small area in front of the windows which was paved as it was above the pavement below. On entering the front door the steps to the upstairs were on view, like most semi detached houses are today.

Our house had a door at the bottom of the stone stairs and no door leading into the living room which in winter made it very cold. So Mum had made a heavy curtain to hang across the opening, this was fixed on to a long curtain pole. It did not keep all the draughts out but it helped.

In my Aunties' house there was a door with glass windows at the top leading from the small vestibule into the living room. In the room itself which was a very large square room, there were two windows and a large fireside range for cooking. The floor, like ours, was of stone slab; every week the coconut matting was taken up and the floor scrubbed with soap and water, a very hard job indeed that Auntie Fanny nearly always did. One door led from the living room into the front room which was at the back of the house, overlooking the back garden. It sounds rather funny the front room being at the back but that's how it was. There was a nice window in there, also a beautiful fireplace with wonderfully coloured tiles in green with all flowers on. Also a large marble fire surround which must have cost a lot of money, even in those days. This room was only used on special Sundays or very special occasions. All the furniture was covered with dust sheets and the carpet on the floor was covered with brown paper so as not to dirty it when walking over it. From the living room there was a long passage, no door just the passage, which you walked on to get to the kitchen at the back. There was a sink with one cold tap, the usual mangle and wash tub and rubbing board. Even though Mum did a bit of washing for my Aunties they washed all the bedding themselves, they had 4 beds, one for each Auntie and Uncle.

The place that filled me with wonder and delight was through a door in this long passage. When you went through the door you were in a bathroom, in those days this really was living it up, to have a bathroom

"... a steep flight of steps to the front door" – Grandad Brook's house at Pudsey.

Photo: Author's collection

and downstairs as well. The room was long and narrow, just long enough for a tremendous old iron and pot bath. The side opposite the taps sloped down like the side of a mountain. It was all fitted round with wood and a little platform at the sloping end. On the wall was a huge gas geyser that was lit with matches and believe me it took half the evening just to get the water hot enough to half fill this huge bath. I used to go down on Friday night and ask if I could have a bath. I was always told 'yes' after everyone else had one, so I got the dirty water but the lovely feeling of sliding down that steep end into the bath and the resulting splash I made was worth all the dirty water. Sometimes the water had gone a bit cold but those were things I put up with because of the pleasure I got out of having a bath in Auntie's bathroom. By the way, I nearly forgot to say, there was no wash basin or toilet, just the bath and the geyser. There again let me explain, this bathroom was downstairs in a small closed in room, no windows or any ventilation unless you left the door open, so if you had a bath when the water was really hot you could not see your feet or legs or anything else hardly for steam. Clouds of steam and walls wet through with water, ah, the joys of using the bathroom in those days.

Upstairs at the end of a long corridor that went right from the front of the house to the back was a small room (the upstairs toilet). I had never before been in a house with a toilet upstairs, none of my friends had them, it was really unheard of in those days. To have one, all to one family, and upstairs into the bargain! Of course there were many houses like that in Pudsey but working class people just could not afford those luxuries. Mind, as I said before, Gran and Grandad Brook had a very large family, 9 children, altogether 11 people, so it had to be a large house for them. Apart from the toilet upstairs there was the front bedroom that held 4 beds and two other bedrooms. One had a very old book case and it was full of books. All these were Sunday School prizes given for good attendance at Valley Road Sunday School where all the 9 children had gone. So over the years there had become a small library of books of all kinds, romance, adventure, travel, everything was on those shelves. Auntie Martha let me borrow one at a time as often as I wanted.

From this small beginning led to another love of mine – reading. We all loved reading, if possible I would have read even whilst eating my meals. I also read a lot in bed during Summer when the nights were long and light, I loved reading in bed flat on my tummy with the book on my pillow.

CHAPTER 4

Mum and Dad

I don't think I have given a description of my mother and father, so here goes. Mum was above medium height, very slim with soft brown hair and grey-blue eyes. She had a very fresh complexion with lots of colour in her cheeks. She had a nice straight nose and a lovely full mouth, nice shaped lips and she smiled a lot. Even though life must have been very hard she was always singing. I can see her now, her sleeves rolled up, her face all flushed, soap suds up to her elbows rubbing clothes on the rubbing board and singing "Jesus loves me this I know".

We were all good eaters so 1 stone of bread a week was baked. Twice a week she kneaded half a stone of flour, that is 7 lbs of flour at a time. Out would come the big stone baking bowl, all yellow glaze inside, and in went the flour, yeast and water, left a few minutes to ferment, then Mum got ready. The bowl was put on the floor and she knelt down beside it to knead the dough. Bong, bong, bong went the bowl on the floor as she pushed and pulled and kneaded the dough until she got it just right. In summer this was a very warm job, she was wet through with perspiration by the time she had finished. No matter how hot the day, if we were short of bread the fire had to be lit and the oven hot ready for the baking. The usual amount was five large pound loaves and one dozen teacakes and also three flat cakes. These were my favourite. The flat cakes were rolled out flat with the rolling pin on the table top, quite large and thin because of course they rose when baking. She used to let me stick my finger in the middle to make a hole, why I don't know because flat cakes or oven cakes I see these days in the shops don't have holes in the middle like ours did. They were then put on the hot oven bottom and baked there till golden brown. My favourite thing was this, spread with either dripping or treacle, my mouth waters even writing about it. My Mum's flat cakes were truly made in heaven. Likewise her Yorkshire Puddings, they were always made in the large loaf tins, four in the oven at a time, covered with onion gravy they were a whole meal in themselves. We did not eat meat very often but on occasions Auntie Martha would bring the remains of the Sunday joint up from their house. She always popped

My dear mother at 18 – Annie Brook.   *Photo: Author's collection*

Mum and Dad (standing) on their wedding day – June 1921.

her head round the door on the way to work early on Monday morning, "Annie, a bit of the cold joint here, make a good stew for the bairns", she would say and put the meat in a paper bag on the table. So perhaps once a week we had a lovely stew done on the fire in a big black iron pan. The meat was cut in small pieces together with carrots, onions, turnip, peas (dried ones) and potatoes and then when it was nearly ready dumplings were put on the top. They rose right out of the pan nearly and were light and fluffy and we loved them. Sometimes we would have liver and onions. Mum used to buy ½lb of liver for about 1/2d, and because there was not enough liver in half a pound for each one of us to have a piece each she would get out the scissors and neatly chop them into lumps (about the size of a lump of sugar). The onions were put in the tin with the liver and then the water, salt and pepper and a little gravy salt. Together with mashed potatoes this too made another good meal. We also had pea soup and dumplings, potatoes and onions done in the oven all crisp and brown on top, and sometimes we had nice rice pudding with lovely brown skin over the top – we would fall out over whose turn it was to have the skin!

So we were fed with good, all home cooked food, no biscuits or cakes, they were unheard of, it was bread, margarine and jam or treacle to finish off with if not full. For a very special treat we did have fish done with parsley sauce in the oven and mashed potatoes. In her life my Mum must have peeled enough potatoes to reach London and back, but we were all healthy and happy and that was what mattered.

One last thing about my Mum, I always knew when she was worried about something or very upset because, without fail, she would start singing "What a friend we have in Jesus, All our sins and griefs to bear, What a privilege to carry everything to God in prayer". Whenever I sing this hymn at Chapel or hear it on 'Songs of Praise' it brings back memories of my mother looking very troubled but still singing and telling God about her troubles.

Dad was, as I have said before, quite different in temperament to her. He was tall and fair with blue eyes and had rather a stern manner to us his children. I have realised since that he was under a great strain in the early days of the marriage when we were all young. As I said before his work was in Bradford at the bottom of Wakefield Road. We had moved to Pudsey as it was the only place where we could get a house. I know he liked Pudsey but he could not afford the money for trains or tram fares from Pudsey to Bradford for work. It would have been too much money out of his wage, so every day he cycled from home to work and back again at night. He started work at 7 am and had to be out of the house by 6 am and did not get home at night till 6.30 or 7 pm. These were long hours and his work was hard so he was very tired when he got home. We had always had our tea and were ready for bed by the time he got home. In winter it was dreadful for him cycling in snow storms, icy roads, fog, and days when it poured down and he came home absolutely wet through; his clothes were then put on the clothes-horse in front of the fire steaming up all the house. Of course the outcome of this was that he suffered a great deal with bad chest colds and back ache. Mum often got very worried about him and as there was no money for the doctor (in those days you had to pay to see the doctor) we had to rely on Grandma's remedies to help him. He always had red flannel, or as it was called 'Doll's Flannel', around his neck and on his chest and always wore a thick broad band of cloth round his back with tapes at the front to fasten it, that was a 'body belt'. He never was without these items of clothing. Gran supplied us with goose grease which was rubbed on back and front. Also we rubbed his back with Sloan's Liniment. He had a bad accident at work and strained a back muscle which kept him off work about six months.

Dad was very strict with us, never ever hit us because he only had to look at the three of us and we knew to behave. No playing of noisy games in the living room if Dad was reading his paper or a book, we went into the kitchen. He could reduce me to tears with just a look or a word, and both my brothers too. I remember a friend of mine was calling for me to go to Sunday School for some event and she said "Will your Dad be in when I call?" I told her he would be so she replied, "Well I'll see you at Chapel then." So with Dad we were very careful to be on our best behaviour at all times. If we had been naughty during the day Mum only had to say, "I'll tell Dad about you when he comes home", and we knew we were in deep trouble.

CHAPTER 5

Pudsey days

At the age of about five I started going to Sunday School at Valley Road Methodist Chapel, alas no longer there. At first I was in the primary class with all the five and six year olds. Our teachers were Miss Crossland and Miss Creasy. Miss Creasy was tall and thin and played the piano, and Miss Crossland was plump and jolly and she stood in front of the class and told us all what to do. We sang hymns like 'If I were a beautiful twinkling star I'd shine on the darkest night' and 'Jesus bids us shine with a pure clear light'. We were taught to say 'Our Father' and lots of other things. I enjoyed it very much, I liked the Sunday School as much as week day school. As I have got older, and now at 67, I realise how important those years were in my life and what a poor start I would have had without the grounding and foundation my parents gave me. We were made to go to Sunday School but it became a great pleasure in our lives and the lessons we learnt there, the good work our teachers did, who gave their time each Sunday for the love of their beliefs, never fail to fill me with gratitude. If only they were here now for me to thank them personally for the good solid ideals they inspired in all who were in their care.

From primary we went into the big school where we sat on rows of forms for all the hymns and morning lessons. At 10.30 we were taken up into the Chapel for the start of the morning service. It was a large Sunday School at Valley Road, about sixty or seventy children attended both morning and afternoon. Many of them also attended the week day school, as Littlemoor was at the top of Valley Road and the Chapel at the bottom. So lots of friends went to both.

The Chapel was our social and focal point of pleasure in those days. We had no picture house at Pudsey until about 1932 when one was opened in Lowtown which was called 'The Palace'. It was here I saw my first movie and talking picture. On special occasions when I had visited my gran and grandad Magson at Sticker Lane, Auntie Mary had taken me to the pictures at the 'Queen's Hall' down Sticker Lane. However this was in the time of the silent pictures and the words came up on the screen. Not being able to read so quickly I had to ask my Auntie to tell

Pudsey Playground today. *Photo: Author's collection*

me what was being said. This rather spoilt it for her and me so I did not go very often.

At Pudsey Town Hall there used to be a music hall. I remember going once or twice with Mum and Dad to this big place with all the chairs in rows. I sat on Dad's knee or I could not have seen the stage. I do remember a number of 'turns' as they were called, one stands out in my memory. The back cloth was the painted scene of an old Water Mill with a big wheel, there was also a bridge and flowers, all in very bright colours. I think it was this colourful back-drop that took my eye. I know the man sang "There's an old mill by the stream Nellie Dean" and I rather wanted to see this Nellie Dean but to my disappointment she never appeared. This then was our entertainment, so you will understand that the social life in the Chapel was very important to all of us.

We had lots of concerts all year round and always a pantomime at Christmas. The choir gave lots of different musicals and we had a very good dramatic group who put on plays. When we had a tea and concert which was always held on a Saturday it was a real treat for everyone. The men would put up the long trestle tables and the seating forms down either side. One table alone sat about 50 people and we always had two of these down the length of the school room. Many times there were

37

two seatings. That was about 100 having tea then getting up and the next lot taking their place. Can you imagine the noise, the excitement and all the hard work that went into making these teas. First of all the ladies on the committee had to make sure all the women baked different things, if possible. We had every kind of bun, tart and cake there was in the 'Be-Ro' book. Then all the sandwiches had to be made, potted meat, salmon paste, boiled ham, plain teacakes, currant teacakes, long buns, scones, you name it we had it at our teas, and all given gladly to help the Church funds. Two huge tea urns stood at the top and bottom of each table with cups and saucers piled in front. The plates, with knives and forks were set at each place and lovely vases of flowers decorated the tables all down the middle. Our teas at Valley Road were a sight for sore eyes. All the children used to go round looking on the tables to see where their favourite buns or cakes were and then when the minister said, "Let's all be seated", there was a mad rush to get to the part of the table you most favoured. Before the tea got served however you all stood and sang 'Be present at our table Lord, be here and everywhere adored, Thy creatures bless and grant that we may feast in paradise with thee'. After that, the beautiful tea. How we all enjoyed it. You see, as I have explained before, we were well fed, never hungry but plain, filling food, nothing fancy. No cakes or buns or things like, so we really loved our teas and concerts. After everyone had eaten and it took quite a long while because of the two sittings, all the ladies who had served the tea refilled the plates and had their meal. So if the tea started at four it was after six thirty before everything was cleared away, the tables taken down, the forms put across the school room by the men, all in lines facing the stage and then we were ready for the concert to begin.

As I got older, when I was twelve, I was asked to join the choir. Practice night was Thursday in the choir vestry. Here we were very well tutored by our choir master, Mr Tom Cooper. He was very strict and we had to be note and word perfect if we were singing the anthem on Sundays. This everyone enjoyed and sometimes I was chosen to sing at the concerts. On one occasion I remember my youngest brother, Basil, was put on the stage with me; he was about one year old at the time and had a large wooden train painted red and black. It was on wheels and he pulled it along with a piece of string. While he sat down with this train I sang a popular song of the time and got a good round of applause.

On Sundays in Summer in the afternoon, after Sunday School, everyone, and I mean everyone, went into Pudsey Park. It was much the

Vera (12 years), Don (6 years) and Basil (6 months) outside their Pudsey home.

Photo: Author's collection

same then as it is today except for the beautiful bandstand which is no longer there. I can see it in my mind's eye, all the girls with lovely summer dresses on. In those days we had dresses of either cotton, linen or crepe-de-Chine (those really were elegant), voile and silk, all in lovely pastel shades. The dresses in the 1920's had been rather short, about calf length but when the 1930's came in all dresses went down to round the ankles. Full skirts that bellowed out when you twirled round. High necks with a small collar and no sleeves. This was the time when slave bangles were very popular, if you did not have either a silver or gold one up your arm you really were out of fashion. Mum could not buy me one but my Aunties and Uncles all clubbed together for my twelfth birthday and bought me a gold one. From the day I got it until well after

I got married, which was when I was twenty one, I wore that gold bangle and never took it off. As a matter of fact as I got older and my arm got fatter it would not go up my arm and I wore it just loose round my wrist. After nine years I had to have it cut off because apart from it being too small to go up my arm it had also got too small to pull over my hand. I was so used to wearing it I never thought it would ever have to come off. During the war I went to work on munitions and was working on a drilling machine and was told it was dangerous to wear it loose round my wrist so I had to have it cut off.

At around the same time as I got the bangle Mum and Dad bought me a gold ring, a signet ring, with my initials on – VM. This I wore for about three years then it suddenly disappeared. Tears and reproaches from my parents for losing it. I looked all over the house, I was sure it was somewhere in there but I found nothing in drawers or cupboards so I eventually gave up hope. About 18 months after losing it Mum got some new linoleum for the back bedroom which was mine and Donald's bedroom. Whilst taking up the old linoleum she noticed something bright between the floorboards against the wall by the window. It was my ring, how overjoyed I was after all that time to have it back on my finger. I promised I would never take it off again and did not, that too had to be cut off!

Around the age of eleven I came into contact with the second gentleman who also had a great impact on my young life. I have told about Mr Threapleton the headmaster at Littlemoor, well the other person was Mr Simeon Myers. He was a well known figure in the wool business in Bradford. He had a large wool warehouse, Myers, Sons. He was also a member of Valley Road Chapel for quite a few years before I became aware of him. A very tall man, very well made, broad shoulders with a fair ruddy complexion and fair, sandy hair and bright twinkling blue eyes. He always dressed immaculately with black morning coat, grey or black pin-striped trousers, white shirt and smart tie, grey spats and a cane with a large silver top. Out of doors he wore a black or grey homburg hat. He had a smile for everyone and the people at Valley Road thought there was no one in the whole of Yorkshire as good as 'Sim' Myers. He had one son, Harry, to his first wife, but at the time I became aware of him he had remarried, about 20 years, and had two sons, Donald and Stuart. My brother Donald was named after Donald Myers. I was first aware of this very large gentleman after a concert where I had sung on stage. After the concert was over he came up to me to say how well I had done and

"Mr Myers ... would take us all for a walk." (The author is second from him on the right). *Photo: Pudsey Civic Society*

would I like to go with him some Sunday, with one or two older children, to a chapel in another part of Pudsey where he was taking the evening service. I was thrilled about this and when he went to ask permission from Mum and Dad I was over the moon. That was the first of a long happy time with Mr Myers and Edna May White, Marjorie Hall, Stanley Coates, Alan Creasey and one or two more. We all went around with Mr Myers when he did his local preaching. We used to stand beside him and sing for the people in the congregation. We all loved it, and him, he was like a second father to us, all the girls used to run up to him to give him a kiss whenever they saw him. He was kind, generous with his time

41

and his money and did so much for so many people at Valley Road. One never-to-be-forgotten Summer he took about 40 children and most of the parents for a week's holiday at Morecambe, he paid for travel, food and accommodation for the whole party. This was the sort of person Sim Myers was. He loved all children and when he became a Sunday School Superintendent he was in charge of the whole Sunday School.

One remarkable change Mr Myers made was on Sunday mornings after Sunday School was over. We all had to go up into the Chapel at 10.30 for the morning service. There were about sixty of us aged between six and fourteen. We did not mind the hymns but sitting still while the sermon was being preached got a little noisy. Some preachers went on for nearly an hour and it was a long time for children to sit and listen. Mr Myers knew this so he persuaded the stewards to let him take us all out of Chapel just before the sermon started, instead of going home he would take us all for a walk. It must have been a marvellous sight outside Valley Road on Sunday mornings about 11.00 when about sixty children, boys and girls of all shapes and sizes all came trooping out on the road with this jolly, good looking man in sole charge. In those days there were very few cars, in fact we never really saw a car at all so the roads were clear. We set off down Valley Road, down into Troydale, then we either went up the road to Farnley and then round into Roker Lane up to Littlemoor Road then back into Valley Road, or we walked from Troydale across the beck bottom following the stream till we came out into Roker Lane and then the usual route home. How we looked forward to this walk on Sunday mornings. Everyone we passed would call out "Good morning, Sim, see you've got the children, it's a lovely morning for a walk". Never ever will I forget those Sundays with Simeon Myers, his goodness and generosity, he always had sweets for us, the time he spent talking to us and telling us of things in the world of which we had no idea. He opened horizons to many girls and boys and his great faith as a Christian and a father made him a very very unique person. Everyone loved him and when he died so many people came to pay their respects that the whole of Valley Road Chapel was full, the church yard full and people lined either side of the road from top to bottom. They gathered to pay their respects to one of the finest men they had ever known. He had also been Mayor of Pudsey so was very respected in the whole town, everyone knew Simeon Myers, he was, and still remains one of the milestones in my life and I shall never forget him.

So, as I have explained, life between weekday school and Sunday School took all our time. On Saturday when I got older I had sixpence pocket money from Auntie Martha which I earned taking the washing down and doing small errands for her. This sixpence I got every Saturday morning. Sometimes I spent 2d on going to the swimming baths which had just been built and opened and was a great benefit to Pudsey.

Also around that time we celebrated the Silver Jubilee of King George and Queen Mary and the opening of the Pudsey playground for children. This also was a marvellous gift to the children of Pudsey by another Pudsey mill magnate, Mr John Benn Ward. He had the playground built, it is still there, just off the market place. When I think of the thousands of children over the years who have enjoyed the playground I think we must have been lucky in Pudsey to have had such good men willing to give time and money to help those not so fortunate as themselves. That playground was opened by the then Duke and Duchess of York who later became King George and Queen Elizabeth. It was a beautiful day when they arrived, the children from all the schools in Pudsey were there to shout and wave their flags. When we all went into the playground after the opening we could not believe our eyes. So much to do and so many rides and a huge lake or paddling pool, full of clean water sparkling in the sunshine. There was a large sandpit full of golden sand, most children had never seen sand before and were fascinated by it. In those days people were too poor to be able to afford to go to the seaside. It is impossible for young people these days when they seem to have everything they want to realise how poor we really were. I have tried in this book to make people realise the poverty in which people lived. We did not moan about community centres, youth clubs, sports centres or anything else because these things were unheard of.

As most children had never seen the sea or sand, it was wonderful in our eyes that there in our own park was sand to play with, make sand pies and castles, put on our bathing suits and paddle in the lake. There were two lots of swings, three different slides, a spider's web that went round, two see-saws, a set of ladders to swing up and down on, a large maypole in the centre with long ropes to sing round on and lots more things. It had a drinking fountain and a refreshment cafe with lawns on either side for people to have picnics on. Seats all round for old people and parents to sit on while watching the children play. It is the best childrens' playground I have ever seen in England. I have been all over in my life on holiday but have never ever seen a playground so well equipped as the one at Pudsey. These days it is not quite the same, the lake has been filled in owing to vandals throwing bottles in. Also the sand pit has had to be filled in for the same reason. However, the other things are still there and one or two new things like the old traction engine which is a great favourite with my Grandson when he comes up here for a visit. My grand-children always ask to go to Pudsey playground when they are up here. So owing to the goodness of John Benn Ward we had something that the big towns like Bradford and Leeds were without.

At the same time as the playground opening, we had a full length wooden dance floor fitted all the length of the promenade in the park. This was all lit up with fairy lights in all colours and a band played every night for a week to celebrate the occasion. My friend Marjorie Hall and I went one night with her Mother. I had asked permission from my parents who had said yes seeing that Mrs Hall was taking Marjorie and me. We were dancing away together, really enjoying ourselves and completely oblivious to the time, when I saw my Dad stood at the edge of the floor. I knew right away I was in trouble by the look on his face. I told Marjorie that I'd have to go. Dad gave me one look, pointed to his watch – it was 10 at night. I started to say that I had no idea it was so late but he pushed me in front of him as we walked out of the park. He took off his shoe and gave me a slap on my bottom with it. That hurt but not as much as the knowledge that he was angry with me and I cried all the way home. I was not allowed to go there again until the Saturday night when all the family went for the final night. What a wonderful week it had been, there again a memory to keep for ever, happy people dancing in the park, all the lovely lights and the band, happy days indeed.

Also around this time when I was twelve, Dad and Mum got the job of caretakers for the Chapel at Valley Road. This was partly through Mr Myers using his influence with the trustees on Mum and Dad's behalf. All our family went to Valley Road so when the job became vacant Mum asked for it. This was not a full time job but Saturdays and Sundays were pretty full days sometimes. Dad had to see to the boiler especially in winter when heating was needed in the school and chapel. Also in the evening there was the billiard room to open up for the members who used it and Dad had to collect the money charged for having a game. On Sundays either Mum or Dad had to be there and stand in the vestibule to give out the hymn books. There was sweeping, dusting and cleaning to be done so it was quite a time consuming job and for not a great deal of money, but as any money was welcome at our house they did the job and were only too glad to have got it. I also helped, it was my job to do all the dusting in the pews for Sunday Service. Taking on this part time job meant Dad did not have very much time to rest. On top of cycling to Bradford and back to work he now had to go out most evenings down to the Chapel to see to the boiler and do other jobs, so he did not get a chance to rest much; it was all work!

Mum did her best, but with three children to feed and look after and all the washing and baking she had to do she also got very tired after a while.

Another thing in those days was the voting. Dad was Labour and very union conscious. He was a union man at work and all done without pay in those days. At voting time in Pudsey during local or general elections not many people voted Labour. I don't know why but it was always the Liberals or Conservatives who got in and to this day it has never changed. Our house was always used as the Labour committee rooms, big posters in the windows with the candidate's name in red. People coming in and out all with their red ribbons in their button holes. We never did get one of 'ours' in, however, I think I am right when I say the first lady candidate for Labour in the borough of Pudsey put up in our ward had our house as her committee rooms.

As I said before Saturday was the big day, baths in the morning and the park or playground in the afternoon. After tea it was Saturday night out. When I think about it now, how the young ones these days would think we were mad. With sixpence in my purse and with my friends, Marjorie and Edna, off we would go. First of all up to the market, a quick look round the stalls all set out in the market place, all with their gas jets ready for lighting when it came dark, the market was open until 10 pm on Saturday nights, summer and winter. Then up to the top of Lidget Hill to the cut price shop that sold boiled sweets. Ten minutes spent there making up our minds what we wanted for 1d. You got a whole big bag of Yorkshire Mixtures for a penny. Then another penny was spent on the tram down to Richardson Lane to the Pavilion Picture House at Stanningley. It was 2d in the front seats, then out again at 8 pm after the first house finished, a walk back up the lane to Pudsey, a last look round the still busy market, then down Radcliffe Lane. On the way home we called in at Glover's fish shop for cake and chips, 2d, and arrived home about 9 pm, tired, happy, full of sweets, cake and chips, no money left out of the sixpence but what a lovely evening, something to look forward to next Saturday.

45

At the age of twelve I got two lovely presents for my birthday, one of which was going to alter my young life for quite a time. For a long while I had longed for a bicycle of my own. Of course we could not afford to buy a new one so Mum had been keeping her ear to the ground in case she heard of one going cheap. A girl at the Chapel had a very good one, a proper bike for a 'young lady'. Mum and Dad went to look at it and bought it. Owing to the fact that we all went to Chapel and our parents knew the people who were selling it, it was agreed that the payments were to be made over a further 2 weeks. So my lovely 'Sunbeam' bike cost 30/- second-hand. Looking back I don't think I have ever had anything that gave me so many hours of pleasure for the price of that bicycle. It was what we called a 'sit up and beg' bike, very upright with the handle bars on a level with your arms so they were outstretched, no bending forward or leaning over. It was just like sitting on a high chair, and as I peddled along I could see just about everything, I loved it. The colour was black with the name 'Sunbeam' written on the frame and a lovely sun with all the golden rays coming from it. There was also a violin case over the chain, it was the guard that stopped your skirt becoming oily and also helped to keep your stockings clean. Also on the back mud guard there were small holes on both sides, and from the holes were strings threaded through, radiating to a round cog fixed on either side of the back wheel. This too was a safeguard for the fairly long dresses and skirts we wore in those days so they did not get caught in the spokes of the wheel and bring you off. This was a very elegant bicycle and I polished it and looked after it like a mother hen with one chick.

On the same birthday I got an autograph book which was something else I had wanted. Whatever happened to all those autograph books we all had in those days? I wonder if anyone has one tucked away, I'd love to read through it. Mine had a leather cover with gold lettering on the front. It was a present from my Aunties and Uncles at Pudsey. Every page was a different colour and all the pages were gold edged. It was very soon half full as all my school friends and relatives put little verses in. I remember writing on the front page – 'Vera is my name, single is my station, Happy is the lucky man who makes the alteration'. All kinds of things were written in these books, loving words, Dad wrote – 'My daughter is a tender plant and I look after her with love and care'. Some were very funny. I wish that I still had the book but somewhere along the years I have lost it. I wonder if the children and young people these days would care for a book like that, somehow I very much doubt it.

CHAPTER 6

Gas lamps and cobbled streets – the world of Sticker Lane

Well, to get back to the bike, having this made it possible for me to get around all over the place and go to places not possible before. One great advantage was that I was able to go on my own to see Grandma Magson at Wilberforce Street at Laisterdyke. This was a lovely change for me. I set off up Littlemoor Road through the town centre on Waterloo Road then on to the main Leeds–Bradford Road to Thornbury where the tram sheds were, then on to Laisterdyke, up Sticker Lane and so to Wilberforce Street and No.67.

At this time there was Gran and Grandad, Auntie Mary and Uncle Albert at home. Auntie Hetty and Dad of course were both married. So if I wanted to stop overnight there was always room for me in the big double bed with Auntie Mary. I often cycled over on Friday afternoon after school and went back Saturday evening ready for Chapel on Sunday morning. I think they all liked having me there with them.

At Friday tea time we had fish and chips for the meal; I never got a fish to myself at home so I enjoyed it very much. Then Gran would look at the clock and say "Go and meet Auntie Mary, she will be coming home now", and I would fly out of the house down Parsonage Road into Sticker Lane.

At ten minutes past five on an evening Sticker Lane resembled a crowd from a football match. You see three of the main mills in the area were situated within a short distance of one another. The biggest was Whitehead's Spinning Mill where Auntie worked. I think every woman who was not married, and quite a few who were, worked there and lived in the long soot-blackened streets with their cobbled roads that led from Sticker Lane. Whitehead's is still there, going strong, and providing employment, but most of the streets with their back to back houses and passages have been destroyed; also the shops we had down Sticker Lane have gone. There was Wilberforce Street, Parsonage Road, St Mary's Road, Lilac Grove Street – this was a real misnomer as there were no lilacs or groves around Sticker Lane in those days. There were no trees or grass to play on, just rows and rows of soot encrusted houses

Sticker Lane with St. John's Church in the distance, 1971.

Photo: Bradford Libraries and Information Service

with smoke pouring from all the chimneys. Gas lamps on street corners and the hard cobbled streets themselves. Further down was Ann Street and Wellington Road and Gay Lane.

I remember the shops and the pubs from Broad Lane bottom. The Prince Albert pub, a shop at the bottom of Wilberforce Street then a small row of shops, the herbalist, two more shops one of which was a sweet shop, then the confectioners, Coultas. Then across Parsonage Road the Post Office and paper shop, the Lion Stores and another small shop, and next to that 'Bonners' shoe shop. At the bottom of St Mary's Road there was a butchery, then further down a shop that sold ladies' things, stockings, hats and blouses. Next to that was the ironmongers, then the Acorn pub. There was Phillip's confectioners, the Golden Lion pub then the bespoke tailors Beckwiths then a big wallpaper shop Cravens. A small off licence and grocery shop at the bottom of Wellington Road. Further down was a sweet shop and then the Queen's Hall picture house and another fish shop. These two shops did very well for custom as people called in to get their sweets before going in the pictures, and when coming out the fish shop did a real trade with people buying fish and chips to eat on the way home.

Opposite these shops was another large mill, Priestley's where Mum had worked. They wove and mended dress goods and mens' suitings, but I don't remember if they had spinning there. This mill is no longer there. Higher up that side was Day's the chemist, another four shops then at the top of Bowling Back Lane there was the Swaine Green Chapel, another chemist and then a very large Co-op and a paper shop. Across was the Swaine Green Tavern then a fish shop, Dennison's, another grocery shop and then the pork shop of Truckenmillers, a shop filled with all kinds of things to eat. The owners were German and had a bit of a rough time during the war. There was the Furnace Inn pub and then Sagars butchers shop and one or two more small shops. So as you can realise down Sticker Lane was everything anyone could wish to buy. A real good variety, something for everyone and most shops kept open till very late Saturday and Friday nights.

The other very large mill was Tankards just down Bowling Back Lane and, as I said, when these three mills finished at 5 pm, hundreds of people were walking up the lane to their homes. Lots of the women wore long black dresses, nearly to their ankles. Most wore black heavy pinafores with tapes round the neck and round the waist and all with a very large pocket right across the front of the pinafore. Also most women wore shawls over the head, all around the shoulders and arms with a big triangle down their backs to keep them warm. These large shawls really were warm as, in most cases they were knitted with wool. Some of the people wore clogs and this added to the noise and excitement in Sticker Lane when these three mills emptied their sheds of people. It was a solid mass coming up Sticker Lane and as I said before the only other thing I can recall like it is seeing a football crowd of today coming away from a match.

Auntie Mary had two friends who worked with her and they all went out together for years. Their names were Doris and Clarrice Haig, they were real friends the three of them.

Sometimes on Friday or Saturday nights Gran and Grandad would take me out after tea, we walked down to Laisterdyke and then half way down Leeds Road where there were even more shops. All well lit up with gas lamps and all open until about 10.30. I had never seen so many shops before as there were down Leeds Road in the early 1930's.

Another thing I recollect from those days was the pie and pea man who came round in the winter evenings, pushing his hand cart. "Pie and peas" he shouted, "bring your pot and I'll give you a lot", and by jove

Map of Laisterdyke 1938.   Courtesy Bradford Libraries and Information Service he did. You got a pint pot full of mushy peas for 2d. Also there was the tingalaree man who pushed his organ up the street, sometimes with a small monkey sitting on the top. He would stop right in the middle and take hold of the handle and the music would come pouring out. All the children came out of the houses and stood around watching him and the monkey. When he finished he came round to the doors with his cap in his hand asking for pennies. The ice cream cart came round as well and you could take your pot out for that and get it filled with lovely home made vanilla ice cream for 2d; it was much better than the insipid stuff they sell as ice cream today.

On Sundays if I happened to be there I saw the Salvation Army come round. They would come marching up the street in a long procession with the drums banging and they would form a circle in the centre of Wilberforce Street. The girls with their tambourines with long ribbons on, the men with trumpets and cornets and drums; they all looked beautiful in the smart uniforms and caps and the ladies in bonnets. How they sang and played, what pleasure they gave to everyone. The Sally Army is still a force to be reckoned with even in this day, and one of the good causes I never fail to give to as they really deserve it.

In Summer I was amazed at the little blobs of gas tar that sprang up like shiny black mushrooms in all the nicks between the cobbles in the street. We used to go and try and get them up into a ball, and then we ended up with gas tar all over our fingers and Gran used lard to get it off. I rather liked the smell of it myself, we did not seem to have these things at Pudsey.

The only people who came round Valley Road was the milk man with the cans of milk on the horse and cart, and the Rington's tea man also with his horse and cart. No ice cream or pie and peas, and definitely never any gas tar either, or indeed, the Salvation Army walking round like they did at Laisterdyke.

On Sundays Grandad always made the dinner, he had a great big black cooking pot and into it went a whole rabbit head as well as half a cow heel and shin beef. Then all the vegetables you could think of, as well as pearl barley and porridge oats. The result was fantastic, I used to eat until my tummy came out like a small balloon.

Where Wilberforce Street crossed with Westbury Street there were four corners and on three of them were shops. A couple of ladies ran one as a home-baked confectioners and a cafe doing meals during the week, and very good they were, real home cooked food. At the other side was a small corner shop which an elderly lady kept. She sold a bit of everything but Gran did not buy from her as she knew she was a money lender. People borrowed money from her but had to repay far more than they had borrowed in the first place. She had rather an oily smile and I did not like her at all. The other shop was the off licence called Wells. Mr & Mrs Wells ran it and they had two sons. Mr Wells was the bane of my young life, he was a big cheerful man, liked a drop of beer, always wore a long brown coat in the shop with his sleeves rolled up. The beer pumps were on the shop counter and he pulled pints or gills or whatever you wanted but you had to take your own jug for it.

Grandad liked a drink with his Sunday dinner so it was my job to go down with the pint jug and get it. Whenever Mr Wells saw me enter the shop he always used to say, "Here she is, the little lass from Pudsey". Then to any other customers in the shop at the time he would say "This little lass comes from Pudsey where the treacle mines are and it's the only place where ducks fly backwards way to keep dust out of their eyes, isn't it love?" Oh I used to get so annoyed with him I could have chucked the jug of beer all over him. I did not realise he was just pulling my leg. "We don't have any treacle mines at Pudsey" I would say and then he would laugh and wink at the other people. "But you do have ducks at Pudsey" he'd laugh. I used to pick up the jug with the beer and walk out determined never to go in there again. Grandad laughed when I told him and he said he was only pulling my leg, but I did not like it.

CHAPTER 7

"Pride is painful!" From wash days to fox fur

On Mondays it was a really special day in Wilberforce Street, it was wash day. As soon as all the workers were off in the morning the mothers started washing. Gran used to take up the hearth rug and the fender and put them away so they did not get splashed by the water she had to bale out of the fire side boiler where the water was getting hot. There would of course be a large fire in the grate all ready for that purpose. Next came two big blankets down out of the attic. All ornaments were lifted off the sideboard and taken upstairs out of harm's way. One of the blankets would be draped over the sideboard to stop it from getting splashed with the soap and water. Next everything came off the piano and the other blanket went over that, the large square table in the centre of the floor had its plush table cover taken off and the oiled cover underneath taken off to reveal the hard white wood top of the table.

After these things were done a very large bowl of hot water from the fire boiler was put onto the table. Gran had her rubber pinny on, sleeves rolled up and the soap and scrubbing brush ready. All the dirty clothes were in a clothes basket on the floor. Where she stood to scrub there was a large piece of linoleum. Every garment out of the basket was scrubbed on the table then put into the large peggy tub in the cellar head. Of course the bowl of water on the table had to be emptied down the sink and filled from the fire place many times before all the clothes were clean and in the tub. Then the rubbing board was put in the tub and all the clothes were given a good rub on this. Then everything was put into the sink, the tub emptied of dirty water, then filled again with clean and back went everything. A good poss round with the possing stick, then garment by garment was put through the mangle and dropped into the basket.

When everything had gone through this process they were put on the table, each garment folded carefully and put through the mangle again and only then were they put out to dry. However any white things like pillow cases or shirts or blouses had to be dipped into Recket's blue to make them come up more white. Then anything like Grandad's best white shirt, or Uncle Albert's, or pillow cases had to be dipped again in a large bowl of Robin's starch to make sure they were stiff when ironed. This was a full morning's work and when all was pegged out on the two lines that went right across the street to the two hooks on the house opposite, and props put in position holding the full lines of washing up in the air, only then did Gran sit down for a pot of tea. On wash day Wilberforce Street was a sight for sore eyes. The lines and lines of washing all across the street from side to side had to be seen to be believed. It was as if the street was all trimmed up for a carnival. All this washing of all colours flying about in the wind. Sometimes however disaster would occur, a cry would start at the bottom of Sticker Lane and would come ringing up "Coal men, coal men". Everyone rushed out and you saw women of all shapes and sizes try to hold two lines of washing up by the props while the men got the horse and cart full of black coal bags underneath the whole lot. The names they got called and the shouts of fury from all sides must have made their faces a bright red if you could have seen them under the layer of coal dust. Sometimes this could happen two or three times during the day because of course all the houses had coal fires and the men were always round. Some came round just selling on the off chance that someone would have run short. So wash day was a hard difficult day for all the women of the street and not many had enough energy to cook a meal at tea-time after their efforts of the day. Sometimes a clothes line would break and all the newly washed clothes would drop on the dirty street. If this happened everyone would help out and each do a few clothes. A great feeling of community spirit held these people together.

As I said before Gran was always called out for births and deaths but if she was not there someone else would do it and the spirit of seeing neighbours and having someone to turn to in times of trouble helped these women a great deal in the hardships they had to endure.

In the early morning during the week we had the knocker-up come round. He had a long pole with a bit of lead at the end and it was his job to see that all the people knocked up were in fact up and awake before he went to the next house. He stood under the bedroom window and tapped on it until Gran got up and pulled back the curtains, then on to the next house. For this service he was paid by each house a few pence a week but he made a wage and was more reliable than a clock. Most people could not afford an alarm clock anyway.

After a wash day came ironing day, quite as tiring as the washing. Mum had two irons she put on the open fire to get hot. No ironing

Washday in Stone Street, off Sticker Lane, 1961.
Photo: Bradford Libraries and Information Service

boards in the those days, just a thick blanket folded on the table top and a sheet on top of that. Mum would wait while one iron got hot, put a cloth on the handle to lift it off the fire, spit on it to make sure it was hot and the hot iron sizzled and the small blob of spit rolled off. Then the iron was put into an ironing slipper, this was a piece of smooth metal shaped like the iron so it fit well, two wire prongs came over the front of the slipper and fastened at the back to hold the iron in place. When you gave a few strokes across the sheet to make sure all was in place and off you went with the clothes. Of course these irons soon got cold so Mum was for ever taking one off the fire and putting it in the slipper and putting the cold one back on the fire. Here again the fire was the means we used to do this job so you can understand why all the houses in the 20's and 30's had fire ranges. The fire was the most important part of the house. It kept you warm, the oven cooked all the meals, the fire was used for boiling the vegetables and the kettle for water for tea. The side boiler was for all hot water used in the house for washing, cleaning, baths and as I have just said all the ironing. Without coal and the miners who got it up from the mines the whole economy of the household would have gone to pot.

Grandma had a charcoal iron, much more efficient than the fire irons that Mum used. As usual the fire was used because the charcoal was made red hot by heating it in a small round steel container fixed at the end of a long rod. You put the charcoal in the little round pot at the end and, with the rod, lifted it in the middle of the fire. When the charcoal got red hot it was taken out of the fire and put into the middle of the iron. This iron was very large and the whole top was on a hinge that lifted up, inside you placed the red hot coal. Down came the top which was fastened at the side to make it secure. There was a funnel at the front to let out the smoke and sometimes the sparks flew out while doing the clothes. This method was a good deal quicker than the fire irons but had that one disadvantage. As I said sometimes the coal got too hot and smoke and sparks flew out of the funnel and fell on the clothes that were being ironed. This could cause a burn on the article and sometimes a hole, so this method had its drawbacks and you had to be very careful.

At the top of Laisterdyke, where the roads cross with Leeds Road, on the right hand side going up Sticker Lane there used to be the Spiritualist Church where Grandma went. She was a great believer in the spirit world and would, I think, have been quite a good medium if she had had time to study it better. However, I can remember going through a small door at the bottom of a narrow flight of steep steps to get into the room where they had the meetings. The ones I went to with Gran always seemed well attended. She mostly took me to social events like teas or concerts. They had a large room with big windows and a large platform. I once remember playing on this platform with some other children and falling off it and knocking out a front tooth. When we could not find it on the floor Gran said I must have swallowed it which rather frightened me at the time. I can recall when a medium visited people handing up to her articles like handkerchiefs and rings belonging to people who had died and then being given messages from them back through the medium. Also they practiced laying on hands to heal people and Gran was very good at this. I can't remember when this church stopped functioning, I wonder if anyone can remember it.

A very great occasion at Wilberforce Street was 'Mumming Night'. This was Old Year's Night. Everyone made or improvised a costume; Auntie Mary had a green and red Irish girl's costume which she wore. Gran made all kinds of different things for me. One year I was a pearly king with buttons all over my coat and Grandad's cloth cap. Another year I was a little black boy like the one on Robertson's jam with a red bow tie and check trousers. Everyone walked down into town, all dressed up, and gathered round the town hall to wait for the clock to strike twelve midnight and then we sang Auld Lang Syne and saw the new year in. The crowds of people were happy, laughing and singing and all full of spirits. There may have been a few who had a bit too much to drink but not drunken louts like today and no muggers or rapists to make you afraid to go out. Those days were very happy, most people were very poor and the enjoyment we had was mostly what we made ourselves.

Just a few words about the fashions in the 1930's. During the 20's I was only young so did not bother much about clothes. I liked getting new dresses that Gran made me but as I was only 8 when we came into the 30's I did not have much interest in the things I wore until I was about 12 years old. One item of clothing I do remember with affection was the long button leggings I wore when younger. These were made of soft leather and had a fleecy lining, wrapped round your leg and had small brown buttons from top to bottom on the outside. On the foot they fit over the top of your shoe and a strap fit under your shoe to keep it in place. We had a small button hook to fasten all the buttons. These leggings were marvellous and warm for winter wear and lasted year after year, they only needed a polish now and again.

Our school uniform in those days was a gym slip with three pleats at the front, a square neck line and a tie belt. Under it I wore a blouse during the summer and a wool jumper during the winter. Underneath was a long vest and a liberty bodice. Everyone wore this second item of clothing in those days, boys as well as girls. It was like a small waistcoat with a fleecy lining and buttons down the front, you put it on in autumn and it was worn every day until the end of May. We had a well known saying "Never cast a clout till May goes out" and no matter how warm the weather Mum would not allow us to take off our warm vests and bodices till the end of May. I also wore a long black pair of ribbed stockings with elastic garters which were made of thin pieces of elastic to fit the top of your legs. As I liked my stockings very straight without wrinkles I suffered agony from sore red welts round my legs at the top. Also we all wore navy blue gym knickers with elastic round the bottom which also left red marks. We had to wear small sailor hats, navy blue velour for winter, both weekdays and Sundays. These also had elastic to fit under the chin to help keep the hat on in windy weather. Altogether these three articles of clothing caused me quite a lot of red marks proving that 'pride is painful'.

Sunny Days! Mother is on the left at the back. *Photo: Author's collection*

In Summer of course we all wore lovely cotton dresses for school and voile and crepe-de-Chine for best, white canvas shoes for school and black strap shoes for best. Dresses in the 1930's were quite long around the ankles until later when they became a little shorter. We had lovely materials for both coats and dresses. I remember a navy blue napper coat with brass buttons down the front I wore one winter and a royal blue velvet dress with a white lace collar to go with it.

There were ladies who did dressmaking in nearly every street and as the materials were very cheap clothes were very good in quality and lasted very well. With having two maiden aunts at Pudsey who were really quite well off for those days they bought or had made lovely coats. I remember Auntie Martha having a grey velour coat with a grey fox collar and cuffs. When she got tired of it she took it along with me to her dressmaker to have it cut down to fit me. I felt like a princess in that silver grey coat. The little fox collar round the neck to keep me warm and the dressmaker made the two cuffs into a muff for my hands which was held in place with a blue cord around my neck.

Around this time for grown ups it was very fashionable to have a plain brown, navy blue or black edge to edge coat in crepe de Chine and with this was worn a flowered dress. Most of the dresses for this outfit were in silk or voile with a white background and flowers of all shades printed on them. With this coat and dress a white fox fur worn over one shoulder was a very smart outfit, and if you had a fox fur, you really were in the height of fashion. To crown it all was a hat. Everyone wore hats when dressed up at the week-end as no outfit was considered complete without a hat. They were nearly all very fine straw ones for summer trimmed with flowers or veiling and perched on top of the head. For winter they were felt or velour with a smart feather. I have tried to paint a picture in words of the dresses we wore and the materials we used. To the young ones of today with their jeans and sneakers, nylon jackets and coats, terylene trousers and skirts and nylon blouses, the materials I have mentioned have probably never been seen. I may be prejudiced but I think the young ones these days have really missed out. Our dresses were so pretty and feminine, you could tell the girls from the boys in my day, you can't today.

Where have all the manufacturers gone who produced top quality dress goods and suitings? Where did everything go wrong? Was it the War that changed our way of living and finished off so many of our designers in the textile and wool trades? If those fabrics were produced these days would the young ones buy them instead of the eternal jeans? When I look back and think that only men wore 'drill' trousers for work; if we had been told then that in years to come the whole nation would be wearing this cheap material on every occasion we would have been horrified.

So my first 12 years were spent in a loving happy home, not much to spend and good plain food, two brothers, Donald and Basil, who I loved very much and still do.

My brother Basil was born when I was 12 years old so I was like a little mother to him. When Mum told me she was expecting another baby I longed for it to be a little sister. I had seen a few pictures at the movies of Shirley Temple with her dimples and her curly hair. I had set my heart on a little sister just like her and she was going to be called Shirley. On the 20th February 1934 I came home from school to find Grandma Magson in the house. Mum was up in the bedroom, Dad at work. I knew my little sister was going to be born. After tea 'he' arrived and Gran said Donald and I could go up and see our new little brother. I was quite upset at the prospect of another brother, I wanted a sister. However we went upstairs to see him in the little cot at the side of Mum's bed. There he lay, little, fat and bald as a coot, not a curl in sight. The only thing about him that impressed me were his lovely blue eyes. He was a real disappointment at first and I made up my mind not to bother with him. However, after a few days I got over my disappointment and he was not really that bald, his hair was so blonde and fine it just did not show much. We named him Basil after the famous Dr Basil Hughes of the Bradford Royal Infirmary. This was because Dad had been in there for a serious operation only the previous year and Dr Hughes was his surgeon. Dad thought him to be a wonderful and kind person so our Basil was named after him. He was a cheerful, happy little soul, always cooing away to himself and I soon loved him as much as my other brother.

So in the year 1935 there I was a happy thirteen year old, contented with my school life, all my friends, my Aunties and Uncles just down the road and my grandparents and other Aunties and Uncles at Laisterdyke. Everything in the garden was lovely in the Spring of 1935 and then the bombshell dropped and my life was turned upside down and things were never to be the same.

CHAPTER 8

"Back to dirty, filthy old Bradford"

As in all families I suppose you are aware if something is going on but no-one is saying anything. This was the feeling I was having round about May 1936. I was aware of heated discussions between Mum and Dad that were suddenly brought to a close if I entered the room. Auntie Martha and Auntie Fanny talking to Mum very intently and then stopping when I appeared. Dad looking very tired and stern, Mum looking upset and a frown on her face, but worst of all, 'What a friend we have in Jesus, all our sins and griefs to bear' being sung nearly every day. Over the years I had come to realise that this was a sure sign that Mum was really upset.

One Saturday after dinner I was getting ready to go into the park when I was told my parents had something to tell me. It sounded rather serious and as Donald was playing out and Basil was in his pram having a sleep outside I presumed that whatever 'it' was I was the culprit. Mum looked at Dad then started to speak to me: 'You know, love, that your father has not been well this winter and he had to have a few weeks off work, well Dr Anderson has advised him to try to find a house nearer his work in Bradford. The long journey on the bike twice a day is making him ill. So Auntie Hetty (Dad's eldest sister) has asked for a house at the end of the row where she lives. The landlord says if we want it we can have it and he wants to know by next week. Tomorrow being Sunday we are all going over to Gran's for dinner then after dinner we will go look at the house which is nearly at the bottom of Bowling Back Lane'. I just could not believe what I was hearing. Leaving Pudsey and going to live in dirty, filthy old Bradford where all there was to see were mills and mill chimneys with smoke pouring out of them all, six days a week. A place where there was no Pudsey park or playground, no trees (I had never seen any trees up Wilberforce Street) or grass to play ball on. What about my school? Littlemoor, I could not leave there and Mr Threapleton and my teachers, Valley Road Sunday School, Mr. Myers and all my friends. The full impact of it hit me like a bath of cold water. This could not be true, it could not be happening to me, but it was. I cried and cried, I could *not go*, I'd stay with Auntie Martha and Auntie Fanny, they would look after me, I would not go and live in dirty old Bradford, I'd die first! Then Dad spoke to me, he knew I was upset but I would get used to the idea. There was a park at Bradford, more than one in fact, there were also swimming baths. Granted there was no children's playground but I would soon be too old for that. 'You will be fourteen in September' he said, 'and will have to get a job and there will be more prospects in Bradford (more mills he meant). You can't stay here, we are a family and we all go together'. And that was the end of my protests. What Dad said was the law in our house and I knew he had already made up his mind we were moving. I also realised that I was not the only one who did not want to go. Mum did not either and that was the cause of the atmosphere I had felt over the previous weeks. Mum had never liked living up Wilberforce Street and as she had spent all her life in Pudsey she did not want to leave. Looking back now I know it was the only thing we could have done. The job Dad did was hard and having to travel on the bike in all weathers was getting him down health-wise. To me at thirteen, it was dreadful leaving everyone I had grown up with, our neighbours, the community at Valley Road, my school, my playmates and friends, it did not bear thinking about. I went upstairs to bed and curled up and wanted to die, instead I fell asleep with all the emotions I had gone through.

Next day, dressed in our Sunday best, we all set off, me pushing Basil in the push chair, Donald holding Dad's hand and Mum walking beside me. We went up New Street, on Smalewell Road down by the railway tunnel, up Tyersal Lane past Tyersal Hall and Chippendale's Farm, over Winnie Hills and across Dick Lane to Wilberforce Street. After a good dinner, where all the talk was about the house and how lucky we were that Auntie Hetty (who was also a tenant of the landlord) had spoken for us and how it could only take Dad about 10 minutes on the bike from the new house, down Bowling Back Lane into Wakefield Road then to Adolfus Street Works, we set off to look at the house. Leaving Donald and Basil with Gran off we went down Wilberforce Street, across Sticker Lane into Parry Lane, from there into Bowling Back Lane past the little tiny church, the Ebenezer, the Artillery Arms pub; across the road was Bowling Back Lane School where Donald would go, and the Farmyard Inn pub. Past Birkshell Lane where the Gas Works were, then Mount Street – at that time a place where police only went in twos as it was such a rough street. Then at the end of Newgate Street there was another little church, St Albans.

Newgate Street – my heart dropped into my shoes. Only a short street about six houses at the front and six at the back, perhaps eight, I just cannot recall the exact number. Stone black-soot encrusted little back to backs with a small cellar head kitchen like Gran's, no garden and a horrible black passage to go through to get to the outside toilet. Goodness knows our house at Pudsey was no palace but compared to these it was heaven. We got the key from Auntie and opened the door. It was the end one of the row and overlooked all the hen-runs and the allotments between our row and the one further down called Lake Row. Incidentally, these two rows of houses were so badly damaged with one of the bombs that fell on Bradford during the war that both rows were demolished and never rebuilt. The people who lived there at the time, including my Auntie, Uncle and Cousin were all in an air-raid shelter – I don't think anyone was killed. After the raid Auntie and Uncle were rehoused on the Bierley Estate off Rooley Lane.

Anyhow, to get back to the house, it had three steps up off the pavement into the house which was square with one window looking into the hen-runs. No kitchen, just a stone sink with a single tap and a small square space at the top of steps that went down into the cellar like Gran's. I remember thinking when I looked down into the dark 'I'll bet it's full of snails like Gran's'. A door in the living room opened out and there were the steps upstairs. One large bedroom over the living room, the other bedroom which I had to share with Donald was half way over the dark passage and was very damp, you could smell the damp in the room. Mum said she did not know how she would fit two single beds in there (we did not have bunk beds in those days) as it was so narrow. We ended up with both beds pushed against the wall, one in front of the other with just enough room for us to get out of bed and walk down the small space between the bed and the other wall.

This then was to be our new home and it was horrible, I never forgot it and never will. I hated Bowling Back Lane, the Gas works that made all the district smell of gas, the soot-grimed houses, the poverty and the unhealthy surroundings. The firm of Tanks and Drums was just across the road from us, and the smell of iron filings and the smell of gas are what I remember of Newgate Street. I think there was a prison in London called Newgate, it can't have been any worse than where we had to live!

I think the rent was about 5/- a week but in comparison with the house at Pudsey it was a disaster. However within a week we had moved in and I can truly say it was the worst time I have ever spent in my life. We did not have time to paper or decorate as it was a case of moving quick to get settled. The fireside range was rusty because it had never been cleaned, it took Mum three weeks to get it clean and the oven working properly. In those three weeks we ate bread that had not been baked properly because the oven had a crack in it and Dad had to try and do something with the oven bottom. After a time at least Mum managed to bake in it. We all hated having to go through the dark passage to the loo, I had to take Donald when the nights got dark as he was too afraid to go on his own. It was pitch black in front of our house, no street light. There was only one and it was at the other end of the row near the main road. Owing to the hen runs in front and the allotments at the side our end of the street was in total darkness.

The one thing that helped me over this terrible period was due to Mr. Threapleton, my headmaster at Littlemoor. When I told him I had to leave the school because I was going to live in Bradford he personally came to our house to see Mum and Dad. He said as I only had four months of school life left (I was fourteen on the 8th September and those days you left straight after your birthday) would they let me travel from Laisterdyke Station on the train to Pudsey Greenside to finish off my schooling at Littlemoor? I pleaded so hard for this myself that Dad said I could as it was the summer and I would not be travelling in the winter dark nights. There were loads of trains in those days from Bradford Exchange Station to Leeds that also went through Pudsey Greenside. The fare for me being under fourteen was 3d return which amounted to 1/3d a week. This in itself was quite a large sum but Auntie Martha, bless her, said she would pay the money so that I could continue at Littlemoor. So there I was every morning setting off about 8 am, walking up Bowling Back Lane along Peace Street, into Sticker Lane, then down the incline to Laisterdyke Station. At Pudsey it was only a short walk from Greenside down New Street into Littlemoor Road, then down Valley Road to the school.

One thing I did miss was coming home at dinner time for my dinner. All my short life I had a lovely warm dinner to go home to, now I had to take sandwiches. There were only two in the whole school who stayed for dinner, me and a girl called Agnes who lived on a farm up Tong Lane. She had to walk to school all her school days from Tong which is a very long way and back at tea time. Not until I stayed did I realise how hard this had been on Agnes all those years. She was a large well-made girl who had it very tough living on a farm where she helped quite a lot with the work. It made me think how lucky I had been to have lived all my 13 years within about 100 yards from the playground. Also all those years Agnes had brought her dinner and eaten it all on her own in the cloakroom as everyone else went home. No school dinners in those days and no transport to take you to school. The children these days don't know the half of it. I can recall Agnes arriving at school about 10 am in winter after walking three hours in the snow to get there and then another three hours to get home. She often looked like a human snowman she was so covered. Also there were no hot drinks or anything like that so we both sat and drank cold water from the tap in the cloakroom. I often wondered what became of Agnes as I left before she did. Also in our day if you were off school even for a day the 'boardman' came around to the door to ask why you were absent and your parents were told off if there was no genuine reason. There were no truants from school in my day like today, you just would not dare play truant or you would get a good hiding from your parents when the boardman came enquiring where you were. So, I sat with Agnes and ate my dinner, drank cold water and got the train home for four months until my birthday.

Weekends were the worst for me, I just did not know where to go. Sometimes I got on my bike and peddled over to Pudsey and saw my friends, went to Valley Road and the Park, but it was not possible for me to go over every Saturday and Sunday. I had to have somewhere to have a meal; Auntie Martha and Auntie Fanny were very good but the weekends were when they liked to go out. After all, they worked in a textile mill as weavers all day long so weekends were the only time to go out. I tried one or two chapels at Bradford, one was the little one at the end of Newgate Street. This was however a branch from 'The Holy Trinity' in Leeds Road, it was Church of England and very high church as they celebrated mass. I was not used to the service and felt out of place so I only went there twice. Another one I went to was Swaine Green Methodist but there again I did not somehow feel 'at home' so after a few Sundays I did not go again. One of the problems was that I had no friends, the girls and boys who lived around all went to the local schools but as I went to Pudsey I never got to know any of them. I felt really alone at this time.

Dad was very content, he was near his work and was back home for tea every night about 1½ hours earlier than before and he did look a lot better. Mum was trying hard to adjust and what with the number of things needing to be done in the house and all the household jobs, she just did not have the time to listen to my moans and groans. Donald had settled at Bowling Back Lane School and seemed quite happy, at least he did not say otherwise. Basil was just his usual happy little self, the move had meant nothing to him, he was too young. So I seemed the odd one out. However, I had found the Wakefield Road Swimming Baths which were quite handy. I crossed Bowling Back Lane, up through what they called The Coke Hills into Neville Road and came out by St. John's Church and the library, the Baths were just above the church. I made good use of both these places. The baths were a source of amazement at first because the changing cubicles were down either side of the pool with just a canvas curtain between you getting undressed and the people in the pool. At Pudsey baths the changing rooms were well away from the pool, the men on one side, the ladies on the other. There was also a rather nice cinema across the road from the church, The Coventry, not very big but very warm with comfortable seats. I remember this with great affection as I did quite a lot of courting there with different boys when I got older. Bowling Park was a little further away but we walked there on Sundays. Also I grew quite fond of visiting Bowling Hall, a wonderful place. I have visited it a lot over the years and always find something fresh to see there. So four of my favourite pastimes were very near for me, but I had to go on my own.

One funny incident occurred at the swimming pool the second time I went, I had bought a lemon two-piece swim suit, 'very trendy' as they say today, the top was not like the bikinis they wear now, it was much more solid, the bottom was really a short pair of pants similar to the boxer shorts of today. Anyhow I felt very trendy in this two piece and it was the first time I had worn it to a swimming pool, I had worn it at the seaside to go in the sea and it had been fine. However, the shorts were held up with elastic and when I dived into the pool from the side the force of the water pulled the shorts down and I nearly lost them altogether, so that was the last time I wore them for swimming at the baths!

I also started going to the Four Square Gospel at Southend Hall down Leeds Road. The hall is still there, not in quite the same splendour as when I started going. It was a memorable experience going there. I remember the first morning I went, all the congregation turned and shook hands with one another, some even kissed each other on the cheek and welcomed each other for the morning service. This really was unusual, and when they started singing the hymns I was even more amazed. Lots of the hymns were those of Methodists John and Charles Wesley, but a lot were sung with choruses which went with a real swing and everyone joined in and some people raised their hands and shouted out 'Hallelujah' and 'Praise the Lord'. They had a very large congregation and choir of young people who all seemed to be enjoying themselves very much. I enjoyed the service and loved the singing so I started to go there and went twice on Sundays for a long as we lived at Newgate Street. I made friends with a lovely girl called Mary, she was a bit older than me and worked in an office in town but she lived quite a long way from me, up Cutler Heights Lane, so I did not see her during the week but she was a friend.

So the months from May to September passed very quickly and it was soon my birthday – 8th September. In those days you left on your birthday, at the end of the week, before school finished, I went round and said goodbye to all my teachers. Buckets of tears from me, I did not want to leave my school, I had so loved it there, the teachers and Mr. Threapleton, and also one or two personal friends who were still there. I promised again and again that I would come back to see them all. I did indeed go back there, four times, the last time was when I was 28 years old and had just had my son John. He was only a few months old when I took him to show the teachers who were still there. Our headmaster had retired by then but I had an invitation to visit his home at Pudsey whenever I came over. So I took John to see Mr & Mrs Threapleton and was made so welcome and they were delighted I had taken John to see them.

CHAPTER 9

"It was decided I should go into mending." Speight's

Before I left school there had been quite a few debates regarding what I was going to do. I had passed my 11+ examinations but no way could I have gone to Pudsey Secondary School. It was out of the question because of money, so I had just gone on getting very good marks at school and I knew my teachers thought I should do office work. Myself, I had always wanted to be a teacher, it was my main ambition, I would have loved it but no way was it possible for me. One of Mum's sisters was a burler and mender and it was through her influence on Mum and Dad that the idea of working in a mill came. In those days burlers and menders were considered quite in the top class of the textile trade. They went to work quite dressed up, even with hats on, never got dirty like the weavers and they sat down all day. They were about the only people with the exception of the warp dressers and twisters who did sit down so that was one advantage.

I did not want to work in the mill but I did not really have much say about the matter. My Auntie had said that after a year being trained I would then earn my own wage and if I was good at the job I could earn as much as 25/- or 30/- a week. This was a fabulous wage for a girl, Dad only got 32/6d a week to keep the lot of us. So with the pressure from Auntie it was decided I should go into mending. Mum made a few enquiries around the mills where we lived and I got an interview at Speight's Mills at the top of Broad Lane, off Sticker Lane. At that time Speight's and the mill at the bottom of Broad Lane called Smiths were both owned by the Bradford wool magnate John Emsley. He also owned Globe Mills and Priestman's which were also in Bradford, in all I think he had five mills. The only thing I can say about Speight's is that mens fine suitings and ladies dress goods were made. The mill at that time was quite new and very modern in lots of ways.

Mother went with me for the interview. Everyone had to go through a small door, entered from Broad Lane, through a passage, on the left of which were the glass windows of the offices. A window marked 'Enquiries' was opened and Mum said we had come to see the mill

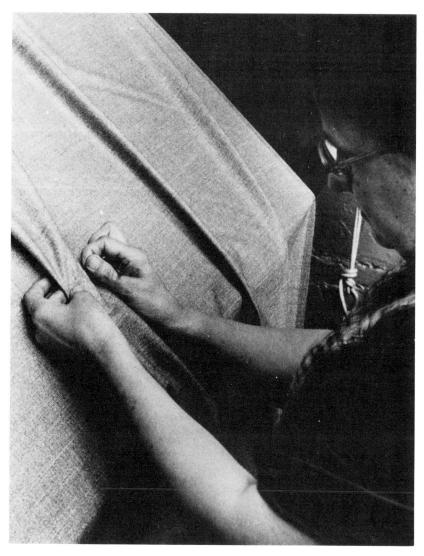

"It was decided I should go into mending." *Photo: Bradford Heritage Recording Unit*

manager. We were asked to wait in the passage where I could hear a terrible loud clanking noise going on somewhere which made talking quite difficult. Mum explained it was the weaving shed which was on the ground floor and not far from where we were stood. After a while this man came and spoke to Mum. I cannot remember much about him but

I do know he asked quite a lot of questions about me. He said that they only had room for two learners in the mending room at that time but would take my name and address and let us know very soon. In the meantime he asked if we would like to see the mending room and the manageress. He escorted us up a very steep flight of steps that were made of wood and looked very greasy. I discovered later that nearly all the wood floors in the mill were in this condition due to the wool used in the pieces when 'in the grey', as it was termed, were impregnated with the natural oil from the wool. Indeed the whole place smelled of wool, a smell I was to become so used to that eventually it was unnoticeable. From the steep steps we found ourselves in a large room full of pieces all rolled up with tickets attached to them in great piles on the floor. The different groups denoted the grades of pieces; I will discuss this later. There were quite a few men in this department and the mill manager explained that these men brought all the woven pieces up out of the sheds, up here to wait to be 'taken in' by the man who did that job, Mr John Dover. We were then taken through another door into a large room which was very light with big windows on two sides. The thing that struck me at the time was the light, and the quietness after the noise of the weaving downstairs. There were 7 or 8 ladies in this room and about 5 girls who looked about my age in two short rows just against the door. When we walked in every head lifted from the work they were doing and I was very conscious of all these eyes on Mum and me.

Telling us to stay where we were the mill manager went into a further room and came back with a very tiny lady who tripped along beside him having great difficulty in keeping up with his long strides. She was introduced to us as Miss Thompson and we were Vera and Mrs Magson. He said he would leave us with her and that she would explain everything to us. She was so tiny I could not take my eyes off her. She had dark hair, brown bespectacled eyes and looked kind and smiled at me and my Mother. She was dressed in a very long pinafore with long sleeves, in fact the pinafore went down to her ankles and was blue in colour, plain with two pockets. I noticed that she too had this smell of wool about her person. After asking Mum one or two things about me she then took us into the main mending room. As we walked through the door I was overwhelmed by the impact of the scene. A large oblong room full of sunlight due to the full length huge windows, again all down one side and across the top of the room. There were, I found out later, about 40 menders at that time working there. Each one was sat at a large mending table on a buffet and nearly all were facing towards the door we had come through. The tables were in straight rows of four across the room and five deep, all in very straight lines. It was really very much like being back at school in the classroom with all the desks in rows, all facing teacher at the front. Instantly forty pairs of eyes lifted up and looked at Mum and me, it was really quite an ordeal. Miss Thompson told us that if I was accepted I would be put with the five other learners in the other room. She explained that the two youngest ones among us had to mash teas for the menders in the morning and go shopping to the local shops for dinners for all the people who worked in the mill. This would take all morning, then in the afternoon I would be taught by her. This would be for the first six months of the work there and I would be paid 10/- a week and the hours were 7.30 to 5.00 every day with three-quarters of an hour at dinner time. After asking where we lived she said I would not have time to go home to dinner as a few did but they had a very good canteen where I could eat my sandwiches. Canteen meals made for you were unheard of in those days, in fact it was very unusual to have a canteen, this really was a great advantage. On Saturday the hours were 7.30 to 12.00 so altogether the hours worked were 48¼, at the rate of 10/- a week that was about 2d an hour. She then said that if I was given the job I would need burling irons and scissors, long thin ones like the pair she showed Mum. Also a pinafore like hers and a packet of size 5 mending needles, a pot for my tea and two mashings a day. With this she shook hands and said she thought I would do very well but would let us know. With that we were taken back down the stairs and outside.

On the Thursday of that week a postcard came asking me to start to work on the Monday morning at 7.30. Mum and Dad were delighted and I must admit that the wage of 10/- a week that I would get would make a great difference to the family budget. So on the Monday morning I was woken at 6.30, I'd never been up so early in my life before, it felt like getting up in the middle of the night as it was still dark. After a drink of tea and a slice of dripping and bread I got my parcel ready. Burlers, scissors, thimble, needles all wrapped in the pinafore. Two mashings of tea and sugar mixed together with a teaspoon of condensed milk in the middle of the tea and sugar, this looked a horrible mess and completely turned me off. I thought I'd never be able to drink the mess, however you live and learn. A small packet of sandwiches which were jam for dinner and I set off at 7.00.

John Smith's Mill, Sticker Lane.   *Photo: Bradford Libraries and Information Service*

It was about twenty minutes walk up Bowling Back Lane into Parry Lane, across Sticker Lane and up Broad Lane. I followed the streams of people walking up Broad Lane. Once again I must explain, there were no buses in those days and the trams only ran on certain roads. There were trams up Leeds Road from town which went to Stanningley. There were also trams up from Wakefield Road to Dudley Hill and Tong Cemetery. There was no transport either up Sticker Lane or Bowling Back Lane so everyone walked to work. Due to the lack of transport people tried to get a job as near to their homes as possible. The hours worked were long anyway so if a fair walk was involved to and from work the days were very long. I set off at 7.00 and arrived home at 5.30, that was a total of 10½ hours a day away from home.

There were two textile mills up Broad Lane, Smith's and Speight's, which both started at 7.30 and I think (though I am not quite sure about this) that the same engines ran both mills for power and light as both the weaving sheds were next to each other on the ground floor. So there were lots of people going in the entrance to each mill. At Speight's we went through the small door, through the corridor where the offices were on the left hand side, big panes of glass between the offices and corridor. In the office stood the mill manager looking at everyone who came through to enter the mill. He stayed there every morning till about 7.40 when he came out and locked the outside door so anyone later than 7.40 was not let in. Also any person coming in even a minute after 7.30 was called into the office by him and given the warning that if they were late again that week it would be deducted from their wage. As everyone walked they could not give the excuse of today that the bus did not turn up, so if you were late it meant that you had not set off in time and that was a real crime. Also in those days every mill had a buzzer which went off for about five minutes before 7.30. All over Bradford you could hear these buzzers in the morning and also at dinner time, this practice was stopped during the war. Each one sounded so different that you got to know the different mills by this method of telling the workforce that they should be well on their way. Some mills started at 7.00, Priestley's down Sticker Lane did, they worked until 8.00 then had half an hour for breakfast and lots of people who lived near the mill went home for this half-hour.

Here I would like to give some details of the inner structure of the working mills in my time:

Mill Manager	– In charge of the whole mill
Weaving Manager	– In charge of everyone in the weaving sheds
	Overlookers and Loom Tuners

	All the Weavers (all women)
	Bobbin Liggers
	Weft Men
	Loom Cleaners and Learners
Mending Manageress –	2 Passers
	1 Percher
	40 Menders and 6 Learners
Warehouse Manager –	Grey Percher
	Finished Percher
	Packers
Warping Manager –	All Warpers and Twisters
	Reaching-in people and sometimes
	Learners
Office Staff –	2 Women Clerks
	1 Wages Clerk
	1 Office boy
	1 Designer
Canteen –	1 Cook (she did no cooking, only
	warmed things up in the oven)
	2 Cleaners for Toilets and Canteen

So everyone knew their place in the textile world, you never spoke to the office staff, they were 'above you'. The Overlookers were more important than Warpers and Twisters, these were all-male jobs. Passers and the Percher in the mending department were one below the Manageress but one above the Menders, all the Menders were above the Weavers – don't ask me why as I never found out!

When I arrived Miss Thompson was there and she showed me where to put my coat. I then put on my pinny and was told to go sit at her table at the very front of the large room till she had time to 'bother with me'. So there I sat on a wooden buffet feeling very shy and out of place. As the women came in they all said 'Good morning Berta' to her. Miss Thompson's name was Roberta but everyone called her 'Berta'. As I said before she was really tiny but as I got to know her over the years I worked there I found she was a real good person, very fair, not harsh. Part of her job was to control about fifty women in two rooms, give all the work out, do all the wage books herself before they went into the office and was asked about everything people had difficulties with. These were things in the pieces we were all mending, she had to make all the decisions about everything, so if any pieces came back from the finished warehouse where all the finished goods were inspected, she 'carried the can' as we say now, or 'the buck stops here'. On occasions she was very busy and I think she kept her temper very well.

I sat from 7.30 until 8.00 when I was taken and introduced to five other young girls, aged 14 or 15 years old. Two of them had just started to earn their own wages after being learners for a year. The other three, Norma, Freda, Marjorie and me were all 14 and just learning. Two of them had been there 6 months so they were going to show Norma and me what to do as we would be taking over the errands they had done for 6 months. We were to go round the whole mending room with Marjorie and Freda to get all the mashings for the breakfast. There were two very large wooden trays with handles at each side which, when full of pots of tea, took both of us all our strength to lift. I went with Freda round one half of the room and she showed me what I had to do: go to a mender, ask her for her mashing which was usually wrapped in newspaper, write her name on a plain part of the paper. If she had her pot in the 'gate' (the gate being the amount of space each table and buffet took up as floor space) the tea went into the pot and then on to the next woman. We were all introduced to each other, this was a real trial for quite a few weeks, trying to remember every name. Some said 'I'm Nellie' or Cissie or Mable but some wanted to be called Mrs Smith, Mrs Grey, Mrs Wood etc. so I had to be very careful to address each one correctly. Also I had to get used to 50 different pots or cups and try to remember which pot went with which face, this caused quite a problem for a week or two. Each tray held about 30 pots. We went down some steps into the canteen, never having been in a works canteen I was most interested in this one. A large oblong room with windows down one side, a polished wood floor, square tables with glass tops for easy cleaning and four wood chairs round each. I soon found out you did not go and sit just at any table, friends sat together and most of the tables had been used for a number of years by long standing employees. So I quickly found out that if I wanted to eat in the canteen I had to wait until everyone was seated and then if there was an empty chair go up and politely ask if I could sit there. This meant that for quite a few months I never sat at the same table two days in a row – some people would be away or not eating in the canteen that day but would be there the next – it was a real merry-go-round!

However, this I will say, Speight's was a fairly new mill when I went there, the mending room with its big long windows with curtains to pull across if the sun got too hot in summer, the windows that opened by way of long cords which had to be pulled, the nice plants all round the room on the window bottoms, the smooth wood floors and the lovely hot pipes round the room that kept us warm in winter. This was the best mending room I ever worked in, and this in a working life in mending rooms for 50 years certainly says something. I never ever worked in a room as good or a mill that had such a good canteen as Speight's, and considering I finished my mending career around 1978 and have worked in 36 or more mills, mending rooms and commission mending rooms I think it deserves mention in this book.

Before I gave up mending in 1978 I was working for one of the largest textile mills in the district, John Foster's Mills of Queensbury. They had a mending room still in use at Greenhill Mills, Florence Street, Leeds Road that was like being back in the 1900's. A large dark room below ground level, a few soot grimed windows that had never been cleaned because they were covered with wire guards on the outside were just on the level of the pavement as you walk on Planetrees Road. No windows in the roof as it was really a cellar. A concrete floor that was coated with dust in summer, no central heating, just big fans that blew the heat out every so often that caused more dust to blow up. The lights were on every day, summer and winter. In summer you never knew what sort of day it was until going out at dinner time. It was like working in a dungeon and just as horrible. No canteen at all, just a geyser for hot water for tea, not even a few tables. You just put your own table top down and ate what you brought surrounded by the pieces you were working on. There were four toilets for about sixty women, it was one of the worst mending rooms I have ever worked in and it is still in use even now in 1989 and the women are working in such surroundings to this day.

Anyway, to get back to Speight's where the canteen was first-rate. There were no meals cooked but there was a lady who warmed things up in a very large gas oven. You could take tins of soup, meat pies, tins of beans or bacon to warm up. We went to the fish shop on Wednesdays and Fridays and we put the fish and chips in to keep warm. Also we had a large iron pan for those people who wanted boiled eggs, we had to write their names on the eggs in pencil to ensure everyone got their own egg back. So they had one of the best canteens I have ever been in for a textile mill and this was of course in 1935.

The breakfast was about 8.30 and after struggling up those stairs with 30 pots of tea on the heavy wooden tray every mender was given her tea but none of us stopped working. You sort of had a bit of bread and a drink of tea but still kept on working. I can see them now, their burling irons in one hand feeling for knots in the piece and a slice of bread or a bun in the other, having to put this down in order to have a drink of tea. If you had an accident on the piece, some of which were white, of course you had a horrible brown stain so off you ran to the toilet to get a rag with cold water on it and try to rub it out before it got too deeply into the cloth. After breakfast we collected all the pots and carried them down to the canteen where they were left for the canteen lady to wash. Back up to the mending room, Freda and I got a piece of writing paper and a pencil. On my paper I was told to put 'Butchers', 'Sweet Shop' and 'Sundries', Freda dealt with the 'Greengrocers' and 'Confectioners'. This prepared we set off together and went round every table in the mending room to ask if anything was wanted. We shopped for everything. Things for dinners like pies and sausages, tea cakes, long buns, bread, buns, cakes and biscuits, cornish pasties, apples, oranges, bananas, eggs, anything anyone wanted we shopped for. You see most of the weavers and menders were married women and had homes to look after and families to feed so they asked us to bring things in for them to take home, it saved them time at night after work. We had four great big straw baskets as there were four of us shopping and sometimes we had to go out twice to get all the stuff. Wednesdays and Fridays were the most frantic as most people had fish and chips, it was a warm cheap dinner – 3d. for fish and chips. The fish shops did not open every day like they do now, Wednesday, Friday and Saturday were the only dinner time openings. We sometimes had list of fish and chips 84 times, then orders for fishcake, cake and chips at 2d. and those who wanted two fish at 4d. All this was to be worked out, change given and ensure everyone got what they ordered. We got commission at the fish shops and we made about 1/- a week from that. Also many of the work people gave us 2d or 3d for ourselves if we had done a lot of shopping for them. In fact these amounts I was given became my spending money, sometimes I had nearly 2/- a week for myself which was riches indeed for me as the most I had ever had for myself was 6d.

On the first day, after dinner, I had to sit with Berta to start my learning. She got a small piece of cloth, pulled out an end and showed me how to hold the mending needle and pick up the stitches, two at a time, then pull the thread through to make it right. Burling and Mending is a really skilled trade. The burling is not too hard to pick up:

Burling and mending. *Photo: Bradford Heritage Recording Unit*

with the scissors in your left hand and a long piece of blue chalk held between the second and third fingers of the right hand, anything wrong in the pieces would be marked with the chalk. All the pieces are done from the reverse side first, not on the face. As you felt all over the cloth with your hands all the knots could be detected in the warp that the warpers had made, the weft knots made by the weavers, and also those made when the bobbin in the shuttle ran out and had to be linked with a fresh one. So all through the piece were weft and warp knots which were lifted out of the cloth with the burlers, each had a little knot with two short ends, our job was to cut close to the knot, then with the fingers gently coax the knot to loosen which left two small curly ends. We had to do this to the whole length of the piece which in those days was about 65 yards long and 60 inches wide. As I said, you did get used to burling and it would not take long for anyone to learn these days.

The mending is where the whole craft of the trade comes in. The threads in the full piece going warp ways are called ends or lengths out; weft ways, which is across the width of the piece are called picks. In those days we did a lot of men's lightweight suitings. This term means cloth that was up to a certain number of ounces per yard of material, so lightweights were suits worn in the summer. Lots of these had mercerised silk threads running the whole length of the cloth, there would be perhaps 2 grey silk ends with a blue or red one in between in the navy blue cloth suit length. Due to the fact that the silk ends had no 'give' in them these broke quite often when in the looms, so if you got a piece of fine suiting, 60 yards long with silk ends in, you knew to look out for the broken ones and these were all to mend. The pieces were normally a 'two and two twill' where you picked up two stitches with your needle, went over two and picked up another two until you had about 26 stitches on your mending needle, you then threaded the needle with the colour of thread that was broken, pulled it through and that was an inch mended, and so it went on until the whole broken end was mended. Sometimes, owing to the failure of the weaver to notice, an end could be out the whole way through a piece of 60 or 75 yards. This was a very time consuming job and it would take a very quick mender about an hour to mend 3 yards, so if the piece was 75 yards long it would take 25 hours of work or even more because you tended to become slower as you became more tired.

However my first afternoon as a learner felt like a year. Never had I sat so long, trying to get the needle into these small spaces in the cloth, I was nearly in tears over it. The 5 o'clock buzzer did eventually sound when everyone put their tools down, took off their pinnies and put on their hats and coats. Berta asked how I had liked my first day, I said it had been alright but this was not true. When I was walking home my eyes were red with weeping and my nose red with all the snuffling and wiping. Mother took one look at my face and did not need to ask how I had got on. I could not eat my tea, I just sat and wept and all I could say was "I am never going back there again. I don't like it, I don't want to be a burler and mender. Can't I do something else?" More tears and then I played my trump card! "I will not live here any more, I'll go live at Grandma Magson's, she won't make me be a burler and mender." Mum had enough sense to leave me alone until Dad got home when he was told the whole story. After his tea he had a good talk with me and told me that everyone felt like that on the first day at work, no matter what the job and also that it was a great difference from the short hours at school to the sudden change to longer hours along with unfamiliar surroundings and people. He understood how I felt but it made no difference as you did not give up after only one day. I had to stick it for at least a month and then we would talk about it again. After this talk with Dad I knew there was nothing I could do but to give it the month trial and no matter how I hated it I would have to do the full month.

To cheer me up Mum suggested as a treat she would take me to the Coventry Picture House to see Norma Shearer and Leslie Howard in *Romeo and Juliet*. I wanted to see this film as we had done bits from it at school, so we got ready and off we went. As everyone knows this is one of the greatest tragedies of Shakespeare, it was beautifully acted but the end had me in floods of tears. So back home we walked, me sobbing my heart out for the second time in one day!

My second morning at work soon arrived, up again at 6.30 to set off for 7.00. I did not mind the mornings, doing the teas and the shopping as it got me out of the mill but I hated the afternoons, sat there trying hard to master the mending part of the job. Norma, Freda and Marjorie were about as fed up as me, so the four of us clung together in our misery and tried to cheer each other up. We talked about our family and friends (I had no friends at that time). These three girls were the first friends I had made since coming from Pudsey. Unfortunately for me they had their own pals they went out with at weekends so I was still at a loose end on Saturday and Sunday. I often went to Pudsey on Saturday for the day and enjoyed seeing all the friends at Valley Road Chapel but as the winter drew on I went less and less.

Donald had settled in at Bowling Back Lane School and had made one or two friends. Unfortunately for me Auntie Hetty's daughter, our cousin Barbara, was Donald's age so was more of a pal for him than me. I spent some very lonely weekends at that time and I was very unhappy. The only joy was going to the pictures, either the Coventry or the Queen's Hall down Sticker Lane, they were the nearest. Even at fourteen I never thought of going into Bradford City centre, young people did not go in our day, we had to be content with what was available in our own district. So for me it was Wakefield Road Library, the swimming baths, the Coventry, Bowling Park for a walk and up to Gran and Grandad's and Southend Hall on Sundays. So life went on and Christmas passed and spring came. I could mend plain pieces and was told I was doing quite well; in March I would have done six months and would get a rise to 12/6d. I looked forward to this as Mum said I could keep the extra 2/6d for myself, this added to the tips I got at work meant I would have about 4/- or a bit more to spend. Pictures cost 4d or 6d depending where you sat and the baths were 2d so I went two or three times a week.

CHAPTER 10

"Thrilled to bits." 6 Cutler Place

Round about April 1937 a great change was in store for us all. One Sunday we had been up at Gran's at Wilberforce Street for our tea and as it was a nice evening Dad said we would have a little walk round instead of going straight home down Wilberforce Street. We said our goodbyes and set off up Parsonage Road, turned right up Dick Lane past Newbould's Bakery and then to the top of Broad Lane. Dad said we would have a look at the cricket field, which is down Broad Lane and is still there to this day. Just a short way down from the top on the left hand side was a short street called Cutler Place where the houses did not start until nearly half way on. They were through stone built terrace houses, seven in all from 2 to 14.

Outside No.6 was a board that stated 'To Let'. Mum saw this and asked to go on and have a look at it. We walked on and I looked through the front windows. What a lovely room, two large windows, long ones with a stone lintel in between them, a good solid front door that opened into the room. Mum liked the look of the house right away. There was a notice on the door that said the keys were at No.2, the first house and all enquiries were to be made there. Mum and I went to enquire at No.2. A very nice middle-aged couple called Mr & Mrs Smith gave Mum the key. We opened the front door into a lovely square room, a good size with these two large windows, alcoves either side of the fireplace – wonder of wonders, a proper room fireplace with a large marble mantle and surround, the infil was green tiles with flowers on all the way down each side. An open fire for coal of course and a hearth of oblong green tiles. I could see Mum thought it a palace and so did I. It was so different from the grubby little place on Newgate Street. We opened the door from the room to the staircase which went up the centre of the house. Another door opened into the kitchen or so we thought – instead it was another large square room with another large window. A large cooking range with a mantle over the top, an alcove at one side of the fireplace and at the other side large cupboards from ceiling to floor. They were really three sets of doors, two at the top that had shelves for pots, pans and crockery, the middle set of doors opened to reveal a large sink with a draining board and heavens above, two taps – hot and cold. We nearly went frantic with excitement, fancy having hot water coming out of a tap in the sink. In all my fourteen years I had never had the luxury of going to the sink, turning on the tap and getting hot water. We were so excited we ran upstairs to see what the bedrooms were like. One lovely large bedroom over the room, another large bedroom over the living room, up another flight of stairs to two attic bedrooms or so we thought. We opened the door to the right hand attic and found a nice roomy attic, sound and dry with a good clear sky-light window. "This will be perfect for the boys", I remember Mum saying. We were both really excited about this house. We opened the other door and heavens above I could not believe my eyes. A small attic, nice and clean with a skylight window but at the end of the room – a *bath* – a bathroom upstairs. Mum shouted for Dad to come up and look what we had found, he was just as surprised as we were and looked at the bath, to us it was the ultimate in luxury living. Back downstairs Mum was appealing to Dad, "Please let's have it Willie, I'd love to live here." A big plus was that she was not slow to point out that it was only five minutes to the mill where I worked, indeed you could see the mill buildings across the field at the back of the house although it was not near enough to be on top of us. There was another short row of houses, Broadlands Street, between us and the mill but it would not be twenty minutes walk for me to work. Also she was not slow to point out that it was much nearer to Gran's and also the school, Tyersal Infants, Junior and Senior school was just a short walk down Dick Lane. The only person who would have further to go was Dad but he had his bike.

"Hold on a minute Annie, we don't know what the rent is going to be a week", said Dad. This did rather bring Mum and me down to earth. We went out the back door, down four steps into our own back garden with some privet and a patch of grass, down two more steps to our own toilet. This also was a first, the very first time we had a toilet for our own use, this put the final nail in for Mum. She told us she was going to ask what the rent was to the rest of us went back into the house. Donald was as excited as I was at the thought of having his own attic bedroom, and the bath next to it. Mum soon came back with the news that the house was 6/- a week including rates. There was a heated discussion between Mum and Dad, I had never seen Mum so determined about anything. Dad always made all decision in our house

6 Cutler Place today. "The heaven we found after Newgate Street."

Photo: Author's collection

but this one time I could see Mum was not giving in. At last she turned to me and said, "Vera, if you continue at Speight's and you get your rise in a week or two we can just afford this house." I would have gladly worked Sundays to get away from Newgate Street, so I gave my support to Mum. She went into No.2 Cutler Place to say we wanted the house, No.6, and would they please tell the landlord the house was now let and we would move in in two weeks time.

So two full weeks after that Sunday night, on the Friday, we moved bag and baggage into 6 Cutler Place, and for us it was the start of three very happy years we were to spend there. Just one slight hitch at the house, all the other houses we had rented had cellar-heads with a sink, this one did not have one. This meant you could go in and shut the door to the living room and have a good wash down, if you could stand the cold. Believe me if you have never had a strip wash in an old stone sink with only a bowl full of warm water and an icy wind blowing up the cellar steps right on to you, you have never lived! We had to run into the living room at Newgate Street and stand in front of the fire in our night clothes until we thawed out. At Cutler Place the sink was in the living room with cupboard doors that covered it from view. However you had to open these doors to use the sink and were in full view of everyone in the living room, which meant all the family. This was no problem in the mornings as Dad was up and washed and on his way before I got up. Mum and I got washed before Donald and Basil got up so that was OK. It was different at night so we had to work out a sort of rota. My brothers were first in bed; at that time Donald was 8 and Basil just 3 years old so they were washed before going to bed in full view of us all. Next Dad would strip to the waist and have his wash and then to bed about 9.30. He got up so early in the mornings and worked so hard nearly all his life that he was usually in bed between 9.30 and 10.00. The living room was then clear for Mum and me to have our wash.

We had lived there about three months when Mum bought an old fashioned wash hand stand from a second hand shop. It was a lovely thing with two drawers for towels and two cupboards in which to keep the chamber pots, the top was black and white marble. After a terrific struggle to get it up two lots of stairs, we got it into the attic bedroom and very nice it looked with a nice wash bowl and matching jug for the hot water that Grandma and Grandad had bought as a present. After that we were fine. One other thing about Cutler Place was our toilet. All our young lives we had to go to the end of a row or through a dark passage to go to a shared toilet. Here we had our very own down at the bottom of the back garden. Oh what joy just to go down your own little garden into your own toilet and not have to hang around if someone was using it. This toilet was a 'tippler'. For those of you who have never used one it worked like this: after use it was flushed from inside the house by pouring water down the sink as there was no water box or chain to pull. This caused quite a bit of confusion the first few days. "Where's the chain for the toilet, Mum?" was a constant cry from Donald who knew there had to be one somewhere but just could not figure out where it was. If you were sat in splendour on the seat in peace and quiet then someone in the house poured a bowl full of water down the sink it gave you quite a start. These toilets did not ice up in winter and there was no danger of burst pipes so it was only a small disadvantage.

We got the front room fixed up with a small carpet square, all clean and new and Dad painted the floor boards around it in dark oak which Mum polished until they shone. We had the piano in there and the sofa and two big upright armchairs which were the fashion in those days; they had been from Mum and Dad's first home at Pudsey. On a Sunday afternoon when Mum lit the fire in the room and it got hot we would go into the front room, this only happened on Sunday or if we had company. In the living room there was the big old square table with a plush cover over it (for after meals), two old fireside chairs and a sideboard. Donald and I never sat on a proper chair as all our activities were done on the table so we always used the wood dining chairs. We played tiddlywinks, snakes and ladders, ludo, did jigsaws, a bit of painting or crayoning in our books and when I read I just propped my book up on the table and sat with elbows on the top. When I see the young ones these days sat on the easy chairs and settee watching TV I think back to my days. I never sat on an easy chair at all and was only allowed to lay out on the couch when ill as Mum could not keep running up and down stairs.

So we were all thrilled to bits with our new house, all for different reasons but we were all happy to have left Newgate Street. I could stay at home until 7.20 in the morning then just run the few yards down Broad Lane and into Speight's Mill, also I could come home for my dinner.

CHAPTER 11

Pieces, passers and perches: mill work

That summer I learnt more about my job and came to rather like it. The pieces were very different and some weeks you did not have the same one twice. The whole work operation went as follows: You had your own table, the top of which was very shiny and smooth due to the oil from the suit lengths being pulled over the top and the rubbing of the menders fingers feeling for the knots. Some tables had initials caved on at the side belonging to menders long since gone. This was done so as to find your own table if they had been moved. There was quite a difference in the height of a table as well, some were quite low for the short ladies and others were much higher, very much like worktops in the modern kitchens we have these days. Obviously a tall girl needed a high table so she was not bending over. When you got your own table it was yours for as long as you worked there and that goes for the buffets as well. Naturally if you had a high table you needed a fairly tall buffet. You had a tin box in which you kept your burlers, scissors, packets of burling needles, chalk and most important of all your wage book. This was just an ordinary paper-back book like a rent book but each page represented a week of work. At the top of each page you put the date of the first day of the week then all the pieces you had done and been paid for. Here is an example:

Vera Magson
May
Monday 21st to Friday 25th

				s.	d.
Piece No.56701	Loom 25	Time On:	Monday 9.30 (5¾ hrs)		
		Time Off:	Monday 4.00		
		Piece Price		2	6
		No of Picks 2			10
Piece No.48725	Loom 72	Time On:	Monday 4.00 (5 hrs)		
		Time Off:	Tuesday 11.30		

and so on until you had gone from Monday to Friday.

All books had to be on Berta's table by 8.00 on Friday so that she could check all the books before they went into the office for the wages clerk to put into the pay packets. We did not pay insurance until eighteen as you could not draw unemployment until then; there was no income tax paid as we did not earn enough. When you had finished your piece your friend helped to roll it up and carry it out of the mending room into the room where the passers were. These were two ladies who had worked there nearly as long as Berta and were both very good burlers and menders. One was called Nellie and the other Mabel. The piece was put down near their tables, the pieces had our initials in white wool. They very carefully went over your piece, yard by yard to make sure all the mending had been done correctly and thoroughly. For mending ends lengthways we got 'beating' which was long lengths of the thread used by the warpers to make the length of the piece. For the picks out and stitchings weft ways you cut a length of the piece from the end, that was the weft, and you used the threads from this to mend everything that went across the piece. When you mended felters, which occurred when the loom and shuttle had made a bit of a mess, both beating and weft were needed to correct these faults, so you had to be very careful to use only the right thread for the weft and warp. If you did not take care the faults showed up after dying (carried out at the dye works) so the pieces were sent back as being faulty in the mending and then you were really in hot water.

On my 15th birthday, after my full year learning, I was told that I would be earning my own wage the following week. This was quite a challenge really because I had been paid 12/6 for the last 6 months and had been able to hand it all over to Mum as I got my spending money from the 1d and 2d I was given through the week for going errands. This of course would stop when I became a mender and two more girls would be set on as learners and take our places. For a week or two we would have to show them the ropes as I had been shown but after that they and Norma and myself would be on our own. I will admit I had great misgivings over this, the thought haunted me that I would not be able to make the 12/6 I gave to Mum as I knew she relied on my wage for both the rent and towards the food. Anyhow, I was helped to find a table to suit as I was very tall and also a buffet to match, and on the Monday morning I started.

There was very little talking in the mending room in those days as everyone was intent on earning money. You kept your head down and if anyone did talk more than was correct Berta soon came up the room and told the culprit to do more work and less talk. On the Friday when my book went into Berta I had made the stupendous sum of 15s 9d. I was thrilled to bits and Berta said I had done very well. When I gave Mum the envelope, unopened, she was so pleased she nearly had a good cry. I never ever opened my wage packet all the time I worked there, it was given to Mum just as I got it. I told Mum I would not be satisfied until I could bring home 20/-, this really was flying high, but, surprisingly enough, before Christmas I was indeed earning 20/- and even 22/- nearly every week. I was quick at the mending part but a certain amount of luck did come into it. You never knew how much work there would be in a piece, some were very well woven as some weavers were much better and more careful than others, so it was a matter of sheer luck as to whether you got a good piece and I did seem to be lucky.

The method of giving work out was as follows: You took out the pieces you had finished and gave it to the passers, Mable and Nellie and then went to Berta to ask for another piece. We then walked into the room where the pieces were inspected as they were brought in from the looms. The man who did this, Mr. John Dover, put each piece over a perch which consisted of two wooden rollers fixed to two long lengths of steel which allowed the wooden rollers to turn quite easily. The pieces were pulled over the rollers and down in front of a large window where there was also a number of lights to use during the dark mornings and winter afternoons. The light from the windows reflected through the cloth and then the 'taker-in' could see all imperfections in the cloth. He did not chalk up knots as that was the menders job to feel for them but did mark all ends that had been broken and were to mend, also all the thick weft and warp that showed up that needed drawing, also picks across the piece that would have to be mended across. So the 'taker-in' had a very important job and Mr. Dover did this job at Speight's all the years of his working life until he retired.

We also had two perches in the mending room for the menders, as some clothes like the dress goods were very thin and the knots were nearly impossible to find by feeling with your hands across the material, they were so tiny, so you used the perch to look through the cloth and the knots could then be seen.

Apart from the passers I have mentioned who passed all the pieces on the tables, we had the main passer, Cis, who was second in command to

Berta. The pieces went from the two passers to her, and she had a perch and a large truck with high wooden sides to it and the cloth went over the rollers; she gave it the final once-over to make sure nothing had been missed by the passers. If she found anything she came to the door of the mending room and shouted, "Vera, just a minute please" and you took your needle, burlers and scissors and beating threads to mend the material down to her perch and stood at the side of the truck and did whatever she had found. After your piece was finished and in the truck that was the end of it and you were always glad to see them in there. When the truck was full of pieces Cis called one of the labourers who wheeled it out into the other room where all the pieces were put through a 'flipping machine' that left them in neat folded piles all ready for the lorries that took them away to be dyed. So as you can see for a length of cloth 70 yards long to be done right it went through quite a lot of different hands. First the weaver, then the weaving overlooker, then the 'taker-in', then on to the mender and passers and finally to Cis.

Anyhow, to get back to where I left off about wanting another piece. There were piles of pieces waiting to be mended, all kept in different piles according to the type of material. On one pile would be the mens coatings or suit lengths, on another a beautiful material I never see these days called a 'venetian', which was a lovely soft material ideal for mens blazers which I think some of the better shops still sell. The blazers were always made from this material, none of this rubbish they call Terylene in those days. We had a very large amount of gaberdine at Speight's, it was all wool and used for mens raincoats. In my young days all men had wool gaberdine raincoats, they were as uniform as the jeans and denims of today but very much smarter. There was also 'trench' raincoats made of wool with square shoulders with the tabs on the top of the shoulders, double breasted with two lots of brown buttons down the front and special tabs and straps on both wrists so the sleeves could be fastened closer in case of very wet weather. These raincoats were also made in the raglan style which was sloped, set-in sleeves and always single breasted which were nearly always worn by the older men. You gave Berta your book and she looked to see what you had just done and it if had been a gaberdine you were given a different one. She looked at the ticket on the piece and put the numbers down in your book and also the price of it. Of course some of the women did not work as hard as others, some were more lucky in their work and some were very quick menders whilst others were better at burling. All this made

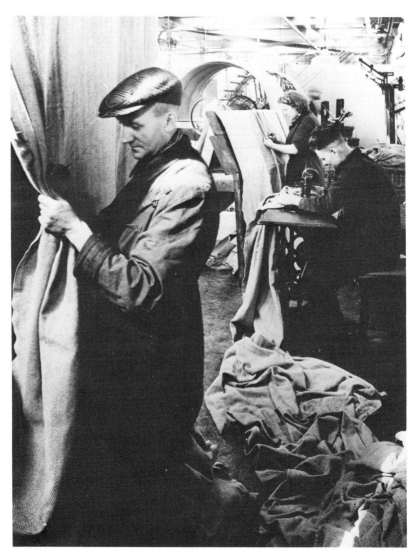

Perching and mending.   *Photo: Bradford Heritage Recording Unit*

a difference to the wage you earned at the end of the week. Personally I was a good mender and very quick having good eye sight. Also I liked doing ends and picks and felters and would time myself on how quickly I could mend in a pick all the way across the piece. However I did not do as well with my burling and sad to say I often got my work back with loads of small blue chalk marks where I had left knots. So all in all it was a challenge but one I enjoyed knowing at the end of the week my wage would reflect just how hard I had worked. At this time my Mum said that everything over 18/- a week I could keep for myself. A lot of the girls just paid 'jock money', they gave their Mums about 12/- or 15/- a week for food and paid for their own clothes, shoes and pleasures. I did not want to do this as I knew my money was really needed.

Another cloth we did was flannel; grey flannel trousers were number one in the fashion parade in those days. If a boy had a navy blue blazer and grey flannels he was really in fashion. The flannel was also lovely for skirts as it kept its shape and looked smart in winter with a jumper and fresh in summer with a lovely cotton blouse. I have not seen an all wool flannel skirt length in a shop for years.

A very difficult cloth to mend was a double plain or satin back, these were a luxury cloth and mostly dyed black and used exclusively for making into businessmen's morning coats or dinner jackets which were always worn with black pin-stripe trousers. Something like the suits you hire today for the groom at a wedding if they are wearing top hat and tails. The tails being the evening jackets that were worn by the upper class for dinners, dances or evening wear.

CHAPTER 12

Singing, dancing and walking – two happy years

I had worked at Speight's about eighteen months and had only seen Mr. John Emsley twice. He always came round to each mill at Christmas when all the workforce came into the canteen and stood around while he gave a short speech and then wished us all a 'merry Christmas and a prosperous New Year'. We all had to reply "Thank you Sir and the same to you." We heard with a good deal of excitement that he was giving a huge dance and buffet supper at the Kings and Queens (Windsor Baths) in the city centre. This splendid 'do' was to celebrate Mr. Emsley's grandson's 21st birthday. When all the rumours were confirmed the place was a buzz of excitement. Everyone talking about what to wear, how they were going to get there and all the other things that to us made it like Cinderella going to the ball. The plans went on for days and it really was a marvellous occasion as all his work people from all the mills were invited. I cannot remember much about that night, how I got there or what I wore but I do remember I had a fabulous time mainly due to a young man I did not know and never saw again who took a fancy to me and asked me to dance. I had never bothered about learning to dance, so I told him I did not know how, but he said he would show me, and show me he did. I danced every dance with him, had my buffet supper with him and walked home with him. He kissed me good night at the door, said he hoped he would see me again sometime and then faded into the night. I never saw him again but he was the reason I started going with one or two other girls up to 'Gledhills' on Westgate on a Saturday afternoon to learn to dance. I don't know if the building is still there but I remember going up a flight of wooden steps outside to get into the building.

Mr. Gledhill and his daughter must have taught thousands of young people to dance in those days. He was a silver haired gentleman, beautifully dressed, about in his sixties. His daughter always wore full length dresses and they would stand in the centre of the dance floor and demonstrate the dances – waltz, quick step or foxtrot – and explain each step then we were expected to get up and try. There were always more girls than boys so you had to make do and dance with another girl but this did not spoil our pleasure. The music (records), the spot lights and coloured lights, the lovely polished wood floor and all the latest tunes to dance to, it was great and I took to it like a duck to water. Even now at nearly 70 I love to have a dance with my husband Leslie, there is nothing nicer than a lovely dreamy waltz or foxtrot played by a good band, even if on records, and dancing with the one person you care for and want to dance with.

In later years I went dancing a lot during the war to the New Victoria Ballroom, now no longer used. The atmosphere was magical, so many boys in uniform, Navy, Army and Air Force, the girls all doing their best to look pretty and feminine in the dresses carefully kept just for dancing. We were short of coupons for clothes, no nylon stockings, if you had a pair of silk ones which cost about 2/- (if you could get them) you were very lucky. We put our hair up in curlers the night before. There were no dancing shoes or evening shoes as we could not spare the coupons for things like that. Despite all the shortages we were pretty, feminine and had lovely hair styles. I wore mine in curls all over the top, the sides swept up and held in place with combs and long and in curls at the back. The page boy hair style was very popular as well. We all went to the pictures to see films starring Betty Grable, Alice Faye and Rita Hayworth, their hair styles were the ones we tried to copy. Looking around these days at the eternal jeans and short cropped hair and untidy, even dirty appearance some girls have I feel glad I was young in the thirties and forties. We were so lucky even though there was the war.

Anyhow, after that little outburst, to get back on the track. Gledhill's taught me to dance and I have had fifty years of enjoyment out of it.

One last thing about Speight's Mill before I finish the tale of my two years there. Before the Second World War everyone took Remembrance Day very seriously. At school we had had assembly in the hall and two minutes silence but it was not until I started work that I realised how much this act of remembrance meant to people. I did not really know what to expect at Speight's on the first November 11th. At about 10.45 Berta came over to where all the learners were at their tables in the smaller room and said that at 10.55 the buzzer would sound inside the mill. We had to stop what we were doing, stay quite still, bow our heads and remain so until the buzzer sounded again at 11.00. It was a very moving experience and one I have never forgotten – this busy mill with all the looms making a fantastic amount of noise then the buzzer sounded and everything stopped, the looms, the weavers, the menders, everyone. Most women in the mending room had lost either husbands, brothers or friends in the war. All had their heads bent and many were in tears. It was only then that I realised the misery and anguish of losing a loved one by war. Little did I think that in just 2 years time we would all be caught up in another war just as horrible and that I would be married to a boy in the Air Force who was sent away to India and Burma to serve his country (but that's another story).

Around this time I did have a loss, two in fact. The first being my very much loved Grandad Magson. He had started with cancer of the bowel about nine months previous and undergone an operation at St. Luke's Hospital. The cancer was too far advanced and even though they had removed the bowel he was sent home to die. Grandma was determined right from the start that she alone was looking after him, so a single bed was brought down into the living room for him and she nursed him night and day for 6 months. During the last few weeks of his life she never got undressed or went to bed. She kept her clothes on and sat in a chair night after night in case he needed her. I don't think there was ever a district nurse called in. The doctor called once a week with pills for the pain he endured but Gran nursed him as she had done loads of other people all her life. When I saw him I prayed for him to die. He had always been so full of life and fun, strong as a horse, loved his food and a pint of beer, a kind word for everyone, and respected by all who knew him. Donald and I missed him most because of his love for us, the stories he told and the songs he sang to me.

I must just remark here that both Donald and I have been interested at times with spiritualism. As I said, Gran went to the spiritualists at the top of Laisterdyke, and Uncle Albert, her youngest son, was a great believer and often went to Chapel at the top of Bowling Old Road. Well, Donald went quite a few times to different places, the mediums were all different people and had never seen him before, or he them, yet they always singled him out. They told him that there was a tall gentleman stood at the back of him with a hand on his shoulder or that a gentleman was trying to get in touch with him from 'the other side' and in every case they all said that the man had only one eye. So as Grandad had only one eye we think that it was him trying to let us know that somewhere on the other side he was still watching over us.

After Grandad died Gran was so weary with the nursing she had done she had a stroke, so my Father broke up the home and brought her to

Laisterdyke (1961), (Queen's Cinema on left).
Photo: Bradford Libraries and Information Service

live with us, which she did for quite some time. Auntie Mary decided
that she would look after her for a few months to give her a change and
while at Auntie's she died in her sleep. I think she just had given her all
to Grandad and after his death she did not want to go on living. So
I lost two very dear grandparents, each very different in their ways –
Grandad outgoing, full of life and fun while Gran was more restrained,
not given to showing her feelings as much yet a person who put helping
others before her own personal wants. They were both very much
missed in the community in which they had lived all their lives, he was
64 when he died and Gran 66 years old.

Coming to terms with death at the age of sixteen was very hard for
me but life went on and something happened that did change things
for me quite a lot. As I have explained I had no close friend of my own
during the previous two years due to the fact that I did not go to school
in Bradford. I had met Mary at the Southend Hall, but after moving to
Cutler Place it was too far to walk all the way down there, especially in
winter. However I got to know a girl only a year older than me who lived
with her parents and brother at the end house on Cutler Place.

95

Cutler Heights Chapel today.   *Photo: Author's collection*

Her name was Hilda Gibson, her Father and Uncle owned the corn mill at the end of Planetrees Road where it joins Bowling Back Lane. They sold hay and cattle feed for hens, rabbits and horses. The building is still there, but I don't know what the business is now. Hilda worked in an office in town and her family were quite nicely off as they say, her Dad had a car, which not many people owned in those days. As a matter of fact the Gibson's car was the first private car I ever had a ride in. Hilda went to Cutler Heights Methodist Chapel, at the top of the junction of Tyersal Lane and Cutler Heights Lane. She was in the choir and one day whilst in conversation I told her I had been in the choir at Valley Road Methodist in Pudsey. She asked if I would like to see the choir master at Cutler Heights, who was called George Carter. He together with his father, Matthew Carter, ran a large coal merchants up Cutler Heights Lane. She made arrangements for me to see him and after the interview he asked me to join the choir as a soprano. So began a long and very happy connection with this small chapel which I remember with much affection to this day. It was, and still is, a very small chapel, very basic with the chapel itself doubling as the Sunday School. There was a small room upstairs for the infants and also a nice square choir vestry with a fireplace and seats all round with a square table in the centre. I remember vividly how welcoming in winter was the large coal fire that was always burning in the fireplace and how lovely and warm the room was. They had a good choir and sometimes there were more people in the choir than in the congregation so during the hymn before the sermon we all filed down from the choir and sat among the congregation facing the pulpit and the preacher. Our vicar, who we shared with Tyersal Chapel and Greenhill Methodist, was called Mr. Alexander Park-Gilbertson. I remember him well as he later conducted my marriage during the war, so I have his name on the marriage certificate. Like a lot of small methodist churches of that time we all shared a vicar, ours lived at the Manse at Greenhill Chapel up Leeds Road.

There were quite a lot of young people at Cutler Heights, all in the age range from 16 to 21 years old, and we had lots of activities all together. Youth Clubs were not known in those days but fellowship and Christian worship was something we all shared. On holidays such as Easter Monday and Whit Monday, we used to go for long walks together. I remember when we all got the train in town from Forster Square to Saltaire, walking down Victoria Road then on the 'Glen Tram', up to the Glen and walking over to Baildon, eating our sandwiches, drinking tea from our flasks and then walking back the opposite way. Sometimes you paired off with a boy or girl but no one broke away from the group to go on their own, we all kept in one large group. Eventually quite a few of the boys and girls did get married and very happy we all were for them.

During the winter, particularly in war time, when it was very cold our normal evening service was held in the afternoon due to the strict blackout regulations. You see, it was quite impossible to cover all the windows with blackout cloth as it would have been too expensive. Also, the older members of the chapel did not like going out at night during the bad weather, hence the afternoon service. However, the youth class (as we were) decided to have a one hour meeting in the choir vestry where there was only one window to be curtained. We gathered there on Sunday evenings at 6.30 to 7.30 when we sang a few hymns and had a talk.

During the summer we set off to one of the parks but this was impossible through the winter months. We all asked our parents if we could all go to each others houses in turn, to have a social evening. These proved to be a great success so if any household had a front room, as mine and Hilda's parents had, it was given over to us for the evening

97

St. John's Church, Swimming Baths and Public Library, Wakefield Road.

Photo: Bradford Libraries and Information Service

and parents kept out. We played games like Charades, Postman's knock, Do or dare, Jacob's ladder and Consequences. How we looked forward to those Sunday evenings. There were of course no picture houses open on a Sunday so we had to make our own entertainment, and we did.

Another thing which became very popular at Cutler Heights were our Moonlight Rambles which I have never come across anywhere else. These were done like this: We looked at the calendar to see which Saturday was nearest the full moon. On that night we met at the chapel at about 10.30–11.00, this was to allow for those who had perhaps been to the pictures in town and had gone home to change into suitable footwear for rambling. These rambles were only held during the summer months; during the war it was double summer time so it was quite light until after 10.00. The whole crowd set off down Tyersal Lane, which was a lane in those days (no Holme Wood Estate then). We walked down to where the road forks left to Pudsey and right at Rothwell's Farm down to Holme Village which in those days was only two or three houses, this was the way we usually went. Up through the village and into Tong. There in the church yard in the moonlight we ate anything we had brought with us, sweets or sandwiches, then we had a short rest being very careful to make no noise. No shouting or screaming out or behaving badly. We were aware that the people of Tong were in bed and we were adult enough to realise they would not want to be disturbed by a lot of noisy teenagers in their church yard so all conversation was conducted in whispers. After a short rest, back the way we had come, we said our goodbyes outside the chapel door with the understanding that we were on our honour to get up in the morning to attend the morning service. If anyone failed to appear they were kidded about it and paid a fine. It all sounds so tame now and it would be to the present generation, but you see I was never allowed to be out late at night. I had to be in the house for 10.00 and there was no trying to get out of it. Dad gave me a key for the back door on my 17th birthday but it was made quite clear to me that if I came in later than 10.00 it would be taken away from me and I would have to be in by 9.30 before Mum and Dad went to bed. I did not question this as I knew better than to go against Dad's wishes. Also even if you went to the pictures the first house finished at 8.30 so there was no excuse. However the Moonlight Rambles with the others from the church were with Dad's approval. He knew who I was with and trusted me, so I did not ever do anything I thought would bring his anger on me.

About this time I met a young man who was to be my first boyfriend. One Sunday afternoon a lady who came to the chapel brought a young man into the Sunday School with her. "I want you all to meet John Stewart Roberts", she said, and then went on to explain he had come

Coventry Cinema, Wakefield Road, 1960.

Photo: Bradford Libraries and Information Service

from Australia where his parents lived to stay with his grandparents to finish his schooling at Salts Grammar School. He was a tall well made boy with dark brown hair and a very fresh complexion, very nice looking, very well mannered but very shy. Of course being viewed by about 20 pairs of eyes he blushed bright red, but was soon put at ease by the boys who introduced him to everyone in turn. His grandparents lived quite near our house just a little way up Cutler Heights Lane past the Chapel, so I often saw him on his way back from school at tea time. He seemed to be always passing the door at Speight's just as we were all coming out after work. Sometimes he had waited for me so I got a certain amount of kidding from my friends at work about this boy friend. We were very happy in each others company, always had lots to discuss and liked one another very much. This did not mean however that we 'dated', we did not, we joined in with the crowd and he became another boy among all the rest. In my young days when you started going out with a boy and it was serious, you first of all took him home to meet your family, and, believe you me, I was going to be sure that the young man I took home to meet James William, my father, would be the boy I was going to marry. No way could I have taken a boy home and then after a few weeks started going out with someone else and invited him home, things did not work that way when you had James William Magson for a father. Funnily enough, it was just a coincidence, but the two boys I like the most during my teenage years were boys called John. There was John Wade from Pudsey and John Roberts, and when I finally found out after eight years of marriage that I was having a baby, right from the beginning I hoped it would be a boy, as I was determined he would be called John. Well I got my son and he was called John Paul. I often think it was due to the memory of these two extremely nice boys I had gone out with when I was young; they both have a very tender place in my heart after all these years. I could not have named my son after two nicer boys and I have been very fortunate as my John has turned out to be a good son in all ways.

He won a place at Aston University in Birmingham after gaining both 'O' and 'A' levels at the Old Carlton Grammar School on Manningham Lane (now no longer there). After four years he qualified as an architect and is now Head Architect for the County of East Hampshire. He lives with his wife Wendy and my two lovely grandchildren Graeme and Charlotte in a little village called Liss in Hampshire. I consider myself very fortunate to have a son who I am extremely proud of because of the way he has worked so hard in his studies and his job. He is also an extremely good father to the children, joining in all their activities and being interested in all the things they do. I thank God for this lovely little happy family of which I am a part.

CHAPTER 13

"I say! You!" Leigh's and the cruel Miss Tailor

So, all in all, these two years at Cutler Heights and Speight's were very happy for me. As always happens in life you get ups and downs, the ups prepare you for the downs, and so it was with me. In the spring of 1939 suddenly we were short of work at the mill. We had been aware for a few weeks that pieces were not coming up out of the weaving as quick, and Berta told us all in the mending that the 'order books' were very low and some of the weavers were on 'short time'. This was very serious for all who worked at the mill. Of course some of the workers who were married were not too upset if their husbands were in work. However, the single people who worked there were very worried. Even those who could 'sign on' were upset as the unemployment money paid in those days was so small no one could manage on it. Being only seventeen years old I could not sign on.

After a few weeks of my wage becoming smaller and smaller Mum and I had a talk about it. As I have explained my wage paid the rent and rates on the house, so I had to have a decent wage. I decided that I would have to leave Speight's and try somewhere else. It was no good going to Smith's as they were also on short time. One solution was to try Leigh Mills at Stanningley. This was an idea as Norma and Freda who were learners with me were also looking for another mill. Norma who lived down Sticker Lane, up Anne Street, had a neighbour called Annie Speight who was a mender at Leigh Mills, and she had told Norma's Mum they had plenty of work and were wanting more menders. It was decided that Annie would ask the manageress if we could go for an interview, so this was set up for the following Monday morning at 10.30. We all three went to see Berta on the Friday afternoon to ask if we could have the Monday morning off. She was very kind and understood it was important for us to leave to get a job somewhere else. She said she was very sorry that we were leaving (if we got on at Leigh Mills) but if things got back to full time she would be only too pleased to have us back. Mills were always keen to retain the people they had trained themselves as different mills had, of course, different ways of training and doing the job. So on Monday morning, with permission from Berta, the three of us got on a tram at Laisterdyke and went down to Stanningley.

At that period Leigh Mills was one of the largest mills in the area, with a large Victorian Warehouse at the bottom of Leeds Road, just below Eastbrook Hall. The building is still there, although not in the same condition as when I first saw it. All the finished work was sent to Leeds Road, before the war, and pieces were sent from there all over the world. The mill made both mens' suitings and dress goods, in fact they made most of the materials that were used in the manufacture of clothes in those days. At the Stanningley Mill they had two separate mending rooms, one solely for mens' heavy suitings, the other for dress goods and lightweight suitings. It was the manageress of this second mending room we were to have our interview with. Even as I am writing this down I can remember my feelings on first seeing Miss Alice Tailor the 'lady' who was going to interview us. We waited in this corridor sat on a bench until she came up to us. We all three stood up on her arrival, and from that first glance of her I knew I would never ever like this person and how right I was. She was of medium height, rather plump but walked very erect with a straight back. Her hair was black and rather frizzy and she wore it in a fringe. Her first words were, "You don't look much like menders to me, how long have you been doing the job?" We all politely said that we had served our apprenticeship for a year and had been on piece work for over a year. She then asked what kind of work we were used to so we told her, ladies dress goods, gaberdines and lightweight clothes, to which she replied we would have a lot more to learn if she set us on. She took down our names and ages and told us that if we were lucky and she decided to set us on, we could forget all we had already learned as her menders had to do things the way she wanted, so we would have to learn her ways. With that she turned round and marched off and left us stood there. To say we were shook rigid is putting it mildly. We had never encountered anyone like Miss Tailor before and I can say now that I have never since met anyone like her (thank God!). We got back on the tram each hoping that we would not be set on. We were all of the same mind that she was a very nasty woman and not a bit like Berta.

I was very quiet when I reached home, but I told Mum my fears about working there. Mum said that I had tried and if nothing further was then I would just have to look elsewhere. On the Wednesday

Leigh Mills, Stanningley.   *Photo: Pudsey Civic Society*

evening, two days after this disaster, a knock came to the door, it was
Annie, the lady who worked at the mill who had asked about the jobs for
us. We asked her in and she told me that Miss Tailor would like me to
report there at the mill on Monday at 7.00. The hours were 7.00 to 5.15
Monday to Friday with half an hour for breakfast and three-quarters of
an hour for lunch, Saturday was 7.00 until 12.00. I had to take burlers
and scissors, and a pot and sandwiches for breakfast and dinner as there
was no canteen there. When Annie had gone I still said I did not want
to work there but Mum said I had to give it a trial for a few weeks and
after all I would be earning my own wage and 'she' couldn't stop me
doing that – little did we know Miss Alice Tailor and what she could and
could not do! Next came the problem of how I was going to get there.
Annie said she went by train from Laisterdyke Station, there was a train
at 6.40 from Bradford that got to Stanningley just in nice time to get to
the mill. As the mill was practically on the railway station this seemed a
good idea, the train home at night was at 5.30 and so it was decided
I should go by train. I worried all the weekend about this change but felt
I had no option, but still knew I was not going to enjoy working for Miss
Tailor (you never called her Alice).

   Monday morning came so off I went down Broad Lane with a heavy
heart. I was quite surprised to find quite a number of people waiting on
the platform at the station. They were men and women who all worked
at Leigh Mills, and over the time I did work there we all got to know

each other very well. It was only 10 minutes to Stanningley and when we got to the mill gates Annie showed us the way through the maze of passages and steps up to the mending room. I had thought the mending room at Speight's large but this was immense, no windows however, only skylights in the roof so it was not as light and bright as Speight's mending room. The brick walls had been white-washed over and in places it was peeling off. It had a stone floor and by the tables were small wooden boards to stand on. The tables were unlike any I have ever seen either before or since in all the years I have worked in different mending rooms. They were just a plain length of wood set in two iron posts, one at each side. This board tilted a bit and you could also push it flat. Under this was a cradle or a deep oblong box and above this was a wooden shelf.

Miss Tailor greeted us with "You're here then" and put all three of us in different places in this large room. There were about 60 menders at that time. All the queer tables were set in lines facing a desk in the middle of the room at the end, near the door and the toilets. Miss Tailor sat at this desk all the time facing all the menders and watching everything. She brought an elderly lady called Elsie to me and told me that Elsie would show me how I was expected to do my work – the way she wanted. She asked to see my needles, the ones with which I mended the pieces. After taking one look at them she put them in her pocket and said they were no good as they were too long for this work and I would have to buy a packet of 'her' needles as she let her menders use only short ones. This was a great set back for all three of us as we were all used to mending with the normal standard needles that most mending departments used. The new needles were very short, nearly like an ordinary sewing needle and we were very handicapped for a few weeks until we got used to them. Elsie showed me how to unroll the piece I had been given and put it on the shelf under the table top. Then instead of sitting down on a buffet to burl the piece and mark all the mending I was told no-one sat down to burl, you had to stand up and if Miss Tailor saw you sat down she came up and shouted at you to stand – charming! So after burling the piece it fell into the box on the floor, you then tried to turn it over in the box and on finding the other end put it on the flat table top and proceeded to fold it up, a yard at a time. Any mending, ends, stitching, felters, thick slubs had to be done the standing and bending over position. Any picks, broken or whole, had to be flipped out and left hanging over the table edge in order for

105

Miss Tailor to see. This way of working was so different to how we had been taught that we all three were completely muddled by it. It felt as if I'd been there a full day before the whistle went for the half hour breakfast time.

I had noticed that everything and everybody had been very quiet but then thought this was perhaps due to me concentrating so much on what Elsie was telling me. However when the whistle sounded for the breakfast, a sudden chorus of voices sounded and I realised that everyone in the mending room had started talking. This was the second lesson in the first hour of working there. Miss Tailor's number one rule was no talking by anyone, anywhere in the room with the exception of herself. You could only speak to each other during breakfast and lunch times, the rest of the time no words were spoken unless someone wanted to ask Miss Tailor about work and then you could only say "Will you look at this please Miss Tailor?" She walked up the room to your table and gave her judgement. However, once or twice during the morning I was astonished to hear outbursts of whispering, everyone seemed to be speaking to their friends on either side and leaning over the table tops to talk to the girls in front. On looking round I saw 'Alice' was not at her desk. The girl in the next gate to me told me that when she went out everyone stops working and has a good talk, but not loud. As I was having a few words with Lily, all of a sudden a middle aged lady on the front row near the exit door shouted 'Lift' and everyone went dead quiet again. I found out at lunch time, whilst talking to some of the younger girls that Alice was the only person, apart from the office staff, allowed to use the lift up to the mending department. So when she went out the women in the front row listened to the sounds of the lift coming up and when they heard the gates shut with a clang they shouted 'Lift' so everyone bent their heads and silence reigned again.

This practice continued for over a year while I was there. Alice Tailor was a spinster of about 36 years old and was a high officer in the St John's Ambulance and was a real nasty person. We had women from 15 up to 60 years of age in our mending room. Women married with grown up children but they were all terrified of her. In the whole room there were about twelve who did face up to her so she did not shout or rave at them. Her favourite pastime was walking up and down the aisles between the tables and then pouncing on some unsuspecting mender who was sat down mending a pick or a felter. "I say, you" was the way she addressed everyone, she never ever spoke your name. "I say, you, what are you doing sitting there? Get on your feet where I can see you and stop wasting time." was a favourite sentence. Sometimes the girl would try and explain she was mending a felter and it was very difficult, but Alice would just take the felter the girl had been working on, look at it and start pulling out threads saying "This is no good, it won't do for me, start all over again." This would reduce most of the women to tears which was exactly what she liked and then she would come out with her favourite saying "The more you cry the less you'll pee." and off she would walk. I was not there more than a few days when I realised that this woman was cruel and delighted in making people cry. Most of the women in the room had gone to work there straight from school so had never worked anywhere else and therefore took it for granted that the conditions in all mending rooms were like that. I really disliked her from the beginning but made up my mind never to let her make me cry. Being very tall even then, much taller than even she was, I soon realised that she did not like having to look up to people when she spoke. That is why she wandered round and picked on girls who were seated. So whenever she came near me when I was seated I stood up and made her look up to talk to me and this she did not like. On occasions she did sneak up on me while I was sat mending something and I'd hear the loud voice "I say, you" but before she could get another word out I would jump up to my feet and look down at her. Everyone from one corner of the room to the other heard every word she said as the room was so quiet and she was so loud! She made me very angry hundreds of times and humiliated me but never ever did I give her the satisfaction of crying in front of her. As I said in fifty years of working in different mills I have never encountered a person like Alice Tailor. She died a long while ago and I often wonder if she regretted her treatment of all those people over all the years she was at Leigh Mills. I feel I have perhaps gone on a bit about this person, but a number of girls who worked there with me had a very unhappy time with her – she certainly would not have got away with it these days.

I have realised since of course that it was the way we were brought up in those days before the war. At school you respected your teachers and did as you were told, also at home parents were very much stricter than today. My own Father was to be obeyed and you did not answer back or give cheek so the people who were over you at work were given the same respect.

We had no canteen, so we took sandwiches, but at lunch time all the young ones went out to the fish shops or the confectioners to get things for dinner. They had no girls to go out shopping as we had done at Speight's. One elderly lady kept a couple of tin boxes under her table from which she sold Mars Bars, Milky Ways or chocolate, if you wanted anything like that. I took sandwiches for my breakfast, but at dinner time went out with one of the girls and got either a meat pie or a cornish pasty, or fish and chips.

There was a door from the mending room that led to the toilets, four of them for sixty menders; the wash basins were in the mending room, there were five basins against one wall, there was no towel you had to keep your own in a bag. There was a rota written on a piece of paper that was pinned to the white-washed wall over the basins and in due course my name went on it. This rota was for cleaning the toilets and wash basins. Every Friday morning two girls had to collect the buckets and mops, fill them with hot soapy water and with floor cloths and bleach go into the toilets to scrub round the toilet pan with the brush, clean the seats, wipe the window ledge and then mop the floor until clean and also wipe all the bulbs in the toilet compartments. After which, out into the mending room to clean the basins, polish the taps and mop the floor under the sinks. This was done every Friday by two girls and we did not get paid for it. All the time your work was being left and it was most unfair but there again it was something that Alice had thought up and the management was evidently overjoyed at getting this done without having to pay a cleaner so they were happy. Needless to say Alice never cleaned the toilets! Every dinner time after eating her dinner she went to the end of the room where all the pieces were piled, made herself a comfortable bed on some of them and had a sleep until the whistle went. If any of the menders went on the pieces for a lie down or a chat they had to talk in whispers so as not to disturb Alice.

Two weeks after starting at Leigh Mills both Freda and Norma left, they could not stand it and were both very unhappy there. I was also unhappy but knew I had to get on and make the best of it as the money was needed. One thing I can say is that the wages were good. The prices for the pieces were not much different from Speights, 1/6 or 1/8 for a plain serge, 2/3 for a fancy dress piece, 2/- for a man's fine shirting and 3/- for a lightweight suiting. The difference was after reckoning up what you had earned, you then consulted a list at the back of your wage book, look where the weekly bonus was and it worked out about the same as you earned. So if your earnings were 10/- you had about 8/- bonus added. So if I got about 15/- which was about average I drew around

28/- per week and sometimes over 30/-, these were very good wages in those days. We did work hard though but had no option with Alice there watching, so I guess she was good for something!

I was filled with amazement on the first Friday morning which was wage time. At Speight's Berta had come round with wage packets, and the amount was written on the front so you did not have to open them to know how much you had made. At about 11.00 Alice came round to each table and flung down a round brass coin with a number on it. These were numbered from 1 to 62 or 63 or however many menders were there. You always got the same number all the time you worked there, mine was 57, as someone had left so I got her number. About 11.30 the door would open and two men came in carrying a very heavy wooden tray, each holding either side; Alice had made room for it on her desk. The tray was about a yard square and had up to 70 holes in the wood which was worn smooth over the long number of years in use. After the men came a woman from the office who was always very smartly dressed, she stood at the side of the desk where the tray was, then sergeant major Tailor took over. "Numbers 1 to 10 form a line" she shouted. Right away the first 10 women ran down to the front of the room, stood to attention in a straight line, number 1 first then 2 and so on to 10. The first woman stepped forward, gave her coin to one of the men who shouted "One" and the office woman took the loose money out of the hole marked One. The woman in the queue put both her hands together in front of her and the coins were then put into her hands, she said "Thank you" turned away, went in front of Alice who ran a pencil through her name on the list she had, and then back down the room to her table. I was astounded, I thought it hilarious to see all these hard working women standing in lines with their hands outstretched to have the money they had worked so hard for tipped into their hands. It did and still does remind me of the scene in 'Oliver Twist' when little Oliver goes up to the front with his bowl to ask for 'more'. I was only 17 but have never forgotten the humiliation of being called by a number and standing there waiting for someone to tip my hard earned money into my hands. This is one aspect of the 'Good Old Days' I prefer to forget but this is how we were treated in those days.

As regards the cloth we mended, some of which I never see these days, we did a lot of heavy serge, this was very good, hard-wearing material mostly used for men's serge trousers and women's skirts. The dress goods were crepe, not crepe de Chine which was a super dress cloth for women; also we did a lot of cloche which was a cloth with a very heavy raised up pattern of roses and flowers, looking as if they had been embroidered on to it. It was dyed in lovely pastel shades and a lot was left white as it was a very popular material for wedding dresses. Indeed my own wedding dress was made out of this cloth. The beauty of it being so heavily embossed was that it could be a very plain style in cut but look so good as it 'hung' very well with it being fairly heavy.

My wedding dress was cut with a high neck, very fitted to below the waist and then flared out to a long train at the back, long tight sleeves with tiny buttons up the arm and little buttons all the way up the back and I wore a pearl choker necklace that just fit the top of the dress at the neck. It was a very simple style but looked very elegant owing to the richness of the material. When I got married I paid for the material by way of coupons, so after the wedding I took the dress to the dressmaker who had made it and she shortened it for me; I had it dyed black and got many years of wear from it as an evening dress or for dances.

At Leigh Mills we also did mens fine suitings and when the war started we were doing all the shirtings, blue for the RAF and khaki for the Army. So the work was varied and interesting. We also did a lot of fine white cloth for Nuns' veilings, the wimple over their heads and the long flowing black veil they wore.

CHAPTER 14

War comes.
Sam and Priestley's

After being at Leigh Mills about four months war was declared on the 3rd September 1939. We had, of course, been expecting it but it was a terrible shock when we heard it over the wireless that Sunday morning. Mum immediately began to make blackout curtains for the living room and bedroom windows. Anything was used, old blankets were a favourite thing as they kept the light from inside shining outside and yet they did not look too bad. Some people even put brown sticky paper over the windows in case they were bombed as this stopped the glass flying all over the place. Everyone had their gas mask and you took it everywhere, you were not allowed in the picture houses unless you had it with you. At work all the skylight windows in the roof were painted black so we never saw daylight from going in to coming out. It may seem funny to remark about it now but all these things, depressing though they were, only made us more determined in our efforts to 'beat Hitler'.

The ordinary people of this time put up with a great deal of which the present generation does not realise. About four years of our lives were really taken away from us and we were deprived of lots of things like sweets, fruit and even food due to the rations. At our house we never ate butter as we could not afford it, but Dad was given bacon because he worked hard. There was no dripping for the chip pan so unless you went to the fish shop chips were out. Also the meat ration was so small we seemed to live on corned beef, made up in cornish pasties or hash. Clothes were in short supply and coupons were very carefully spent. Even going to work on the train was different. All the carriages were blacked out, the windows painted black and the light bulbs were painted over, leaving only one small spot of light shining down into the compartments. This was not too bad during September and October but when the winter months arrived it was dreadful. Waiting on Laisterdyke platform for the train to arrive to take us to Stanningley, we all crowded into the waiting room which I recall with much regrets for times long passed. It was a long room with a huge table down the centre and

"... we all crowded into the waiting room." Laisterdyke Station, 1967.

Photo: Telegraph & Argus

long bench seats on three sides, a door in the end wall and the fireplace in the other end wall. This fireplace was always lit and a lovely fire burning, no matter what time of day you were in the room. All the windows of course were painted over so no light was visible outside. We all huddled round the lovely warm fire trying to get warm after a 20 minute walk in the cold and snow; that waiting room was a 'God-send'.

We were all put on a rota at the mill and after a day's work, every so often, you had to stay all night with about four other girls and 'fire watch'. The older women who had husbands and children to look after were exempt from this job but the young ones like me had to do their bit. This involved wearing a tin hat, learning how to use a stirrup pump and water or sand, just in case an incendiary bomb dropped on the mending room roof. All this put a great deal of pressure on everyone and we were all aware of the seriousness of our efforts. When the warning came by way of sirens sounding out everyone knew what to do. We did not have many daylight raids, they were mainly at night, moonlit nights were the worst. Everyone was aware when it got near to the full moon

Priesley's Mill, Laisterdyke, 1961. *Photo: Bradford Libraries and Information Service*

and we were all 'geared up' and waiting.

One good thing to come out of the war was that we 'got rid' of Alice Tailor! As she was an officer in the St. John's Ambulance she was called up pretty quickly into the nursing service. The day she finished we had quite a celebration as Elsie, who was a much nicer person, was put in her place. However we had not seen the last of Alice. When on leave she always came into the mill and such was her influence over us we all fell silent as soon as she walked through the door. She looked very smart in the uniform of black suit with a white blouse, a tricorne hat with a badge on the side, flat black shoes and a red tie. She marched down the room of tables like the Queen on a tour. She stopped at each table and had a few words with everyone. It was the only time I ever saw her behave as a human being and was the only time she ever called me by my name, "And how are you Vera?" "Very well thank you Alice" and on she swept to the next table. It was indeed like being visited by royalty.

Of course, with the war starting all industry got geared up to the war effort. Most of the mills got on full time, turning out hundred and thousands of yards of khaki, air force blue and navy blue materials for

113

the lads in the forces. There were also the fire brigades and the men doing the Air Raid Precautions (ARP) to fit with uniforms. All the services needed shirts, boots, stockings and underwear so the whole clothing industry was put into top gear to provide our men with what was needed. Suddenly, all the mills were wanting women workers, so I decided I'd had enough at Leigh Mills and travelling all that way. Writing of travelling, I will just put in this funny incident. One morning just before Christmas it was a very dark, dismal morning and everyone was waiting for the train, but due to the bit of fog the train was a few minutes late. When it arrived there was a mad rush to get in the carriages. I opened a door and sat down on what I though to be an empty seat next to the window, I sat right down on the lap of a gentleman who was already sat there. I felt a real fool but it got quite a laugh from the other people in the compartment. After that I was very careful to look where I was going to sit.

Anyway, to get back to the mills. I went to the manager at Speight's to ask for a job back at the mending room. He said he was sorry but they were full up in the mending department, all the tables taken, but the first vacancy they had I could have it. This really upset me as I had looked forward to seeing Berta and lots of old friends there. This then presented me with another dilemma – where next? Mum suggested I try Priestley's down by the Queen's Hall Cinema down Sticker Lane. She had worked there as a weaver before I was born and it was quite near. So down I went for an interview. The mill manager was a man called Claude who had lost an arm in the 1914–18 war, he did not wear a false arm, just had his sleeve hanging loose pinned to his jacket. After a few questions about where I had learned the job and what I had been doing at Leigh Mills he set me on.

Priestley's was an old mill and was full of queer little rooms all over the place. The weaving shed was large, but the mending rooms consisted of one fairly big room and two or three very small rooms that took about 8 or 10 menders and a passer in charge. I was put in a small room, very dark and dingy with no windows to the outside so the lights had to be on all the day long. All the other women were years older than me, most of them married with husbands in the forces. Two were spinster sisters, Sally and Nellie and they were the only two who seemed to talk. Sally was a jolly, rotund lady who had a good sense of humour and if it hadn't been for her I don't think I could have put up with it for long. Once again it was a totally different way of working.

The tables were as I had been used to at Speight's and the burling needles were the normal length but the way of doing the job was different. Annie, who was in charge, gave out the work, and also passed it to make sure it was correct. She was a nice, quiet, pleasant lady but very much afraid of Claude. When he came in the room it was like being back with Alice Tailor. You could not speak if he was around and he watched everyone while pretending to talk to Annie. One advantage was I could go home at breakfast time, 8.00 to 8.30; it was a bit of a rush but worth it to get away from the confined feeling of working in so small a room. I could also get home for dinner and sooner at tea time. I did not like the mill, it was so very old and cramped; also, having three mending rooms and so many different people in charge made things difficult. Although Annie was in charge of the room and the menders she could not make any decisions without consulting Claude. This was very bad because sometimes she could not find him, so had to go all round the mill just to ask him some question about a piece that she could really have sorted out herself. This in turn held us up in our work so made us waste a lot of time which meant money when you were earning your own wage.

I soon got into the habit of singing very softly to myself the latest tunes from the films. The other women must have liked listening to me as they soon asked me to sing a few songs for them. Those who had husbands serving away from home always chose the same songs so I became quite an expert in singing 'I'll be loving you always', 'I never said thanks for that lovely weekend', 'Once in a while', 'The white cliffs of Dover', 'A nightingale sang in Berkley Square', 'Moonlight becomes you', 'Coming in on a wing and a prayer' and 'I'll see you again' which was the number one favourite. One day Annie came up to my table and said she had something to tell me. She looked so upset and red in the face I could not think what I'd done. However she said Claude had been passing outside our room and heard me singing, he had told her that people could not sing and work at the same time so he did not want any more singing. We were all struck dumb with surprise and I was very angry. The next time I saw Claude I asked him why he had not told me to my face, he spluttered and coughed and made the lame excuse that if one person started singing everyone would be doing it. I told him that singing had cheered a lot of the mender's up and if they wanted me to sing, then sing I would. This was only the first of quite a few 'do's' with Claude so I think he considered me to be a trouble-maker.

During this period of unrest at work, my home and personal life was having a bit of a shake up. For a long time I had been quite friendly with a boy called Sam. I had often seen him, over a number of years, riding about on his bike and also at the swimming baths. He did not attend our Chapel so I never saw him at weekends. However, one Thursday evening about 6.00 (it was just before Christmas and very dark) I had been to the Post Office at the bottom of Parsonage Road. Sam was outside and we began talking, he said he would walk me back home and I was quite surprised at the offer. Before he left me we made a 'date' for Saturday night – 6.30 at the bottom of Broad Lane. When I arrived Sam was stood waiting, very smart he looked too with a nice navy blue suit, white shirt and a lovely navy blue overcoat and a white scarf round his neck. It was a very cold night so we decided to go to the Coventry Picture House down Wakefield Road. It was a 20 minute walk down Parry Lane and then across Neville Road which brings you out by St John's Church, then over the road to the Coventry. This was a lovely little picture house, very small and always lovely and warm, the seats were all plush tip up ones, which was not always the case in all picture houses before the war. There was a small central block of seats downstairs with the aisles down each side. Upstairs there was a small balcony with seats on either side of a central aisle. Also upstairs there were twin seats for courting couples or anyone else if that's what they preferred. These were very popular with young couples, they could sit close to each other as there was no chair arm between them, so the boy could put his arm around you and cuddle up close (very nice if you were with someone you really liked). It was left up to the girl to choose whether to sit in the double seats or not, it all depended on who you were with and how much you liked and trusted them!

This being my first date with Sam I steered away from the double seats. The price by the way for seats in the balcony was 9d each (nearly 5p today). For this you got a three-hour programme of news, a short second feature film and the main film; so you can understand why we went to the pictures for a night out, it was warm, comfortable and a good three hours entertainment. We both enjoyed the programme and when we had seen the whole show we came out about 9.45. I told Sam we would have to walk home very quickly as I had to be in by 10.00. It was a very cold frosty night and by the time we had reached my house we were both a bit out of breath. I opened the back door and on impulse did something I had never done before – I said "Come in Sam, just for a minute while I tell Mum I am in." I usually said my good-byes at the end of the street. Sam had been a 'nice' date, no trouble with him in the pictures wanting to 'neck' as they say these days. I shut the back door, switched on the light in the living room, poked the coal fire to warm up the room then went to the bottom of the stairs and shouted, "Mum, I'm back", to which she replied for me not to be long before coming to bed and not to put any coal on the fire. I closed the door, smiled at Sam and thanked him for a nice evening. He asked me if I would like to go again and I said I would. I switched off the light before opening the door to let him out, but as I opened the door I could just make out the figure of someone opening our back gate. In that split second I knew it was Dad and I went into complete shock. What was Dad doing out of bed at 10.15 but more to the point what would he say on seeing Sam in the house? I had never brought a boy home before on his own. We had the boys and girls from the Chapel on Sunday evenings, but it had always been impressed upon me that I only brought a young man back if it was 'serious' and we were courting. All this flashed through my mind and suddenly my legs felt as if they were going to let me drop. The toilet was outside by the garden gate and I heard Dad say "Will be in in a minute, just going to the toilet." I pushed the door to, put on the light, grabbed Sam's hand, pulled him across the living room, opened the door to the cellar, pulled him down the steps after me, opened the wood door to the coal cellar, shoved him in, shut the door, put on the bolt and raced upstairs just in time to see Dad come through the door. "I thought you were in bed" I said. "No, I had a walk up to Auntie Mary's" (his sister who lived on Tong Street) "and stayed longer than I meant to." I asked him if he wanted a pot of tea or a sandwich, he said he had his supper and I was to go to bed as it was late. So I went to bed. I heard Dad come up and him and Mum talking, I was rigid with fear and pity for Sam in the coal cellar. How could I get him out? I got up and crept to the top of the stairs. "Is that you Vera? What are you doing?" "I feel a bit sick Mum", (very true) "and I want a drink of water." Now if the bathroom had been on the first floor I could not have made that excuse but as it was in one of the attics and the boys were sleeping up there, it was quite natural for me to go downstairs. Down I flew in my nightie, no slippers on, and very quietly opened the door to the cellar, switched on the light and flew down the steps. On opening the door all I could see of Sam was his white scarf round his neck as he sat there on a lump of coal. "Hurry up"

I whispered as I grabbed his hand again, raced up the steps, across the living room and gently opened the back door with the key. I pushed Sam out into the dark, shut the door, turned the key, had a drink of water, fled upstairs and into bed. I remember thinking before I went to sleep, that would be the last I saw of Sam and I rather liked him. It was not the last of Sam as we met again and began going out together quite often. We often had a laugh over that first date when he finished the evening sat on a lump of coal in our cellar!

A few months later Mum found another house. We had all loved living at No.6 Cutler Place but it was rather a hard house to follow with a lot of steps at the back and two lots of stairs inside. Our new house was at 21 Beverley Street, one of the long rows of through terraced houses at the top, left-hand side of Parsonage Road. It was a nice house but did not have a front room like No.6. There was a large living room with a cooking range. The front door led to the garden in front, there were two other doors in the room, both next to each other. One led into the kitchen, the other to the stairs and bedrooms. The kitchen was nice and square with an old set pot boiler in the corner, the bath was also in there and it had a big wooden lid over it which made it like a worktop which was very handy. Under the window was the sink, hot and cold water, then the door to the back garden and another door to a small pantry that was under the stairs. Upstairs there was a very big front bedroom and also a smaller one, then up to the attic which was an all-over one, not divided like Cutler Place, the boys were to sleep there. This house was 4/6 a week so was cheaper than our last one, as every shilling counted in those days it was quite a bargain. The landlord called once a month to collect the rents, he owned about eight houses all next to each other. So once again we moved. Donald was even nearer school as Tyersal School was at the end of the street, it was also handy for Basil who had just started in the infants. It was also nearer to me working at Priestley's so I reached home much quicker at breakfast and dinner time.

CHAPTER 15

War rations and war effort. Munitions and marriage

I still did not like working at Priestley's and felt I should be doing more for the war effort. One or two of the boys from the chapel had been called up into the Navy and Army. One of the girls had joined the WRNS and two had gone in the Land Army. I was a bit handicapped as I was in a reserved occupation as textiles and engineering were both needed for the war effort. I did not want to go away from home as I knew the money I earned was still needed, more so now that Donald and Basil were growing and needed more food and clothes. Dad had joined the Railway Home Guard and put in a couple of hours training per week. I think everyone was aware that the Germans would try to land here and so everyone wanted to do 'their bit' to help. The Mums and Grannies had their share of queuing outside shops for food and having to plan good meals with the food that was to hand. Everyone turned their gardens into allotments if they were big enough and the people who lived near open land were encouraged to keep hens for eggs. We only got one egg each a week, and dried egg was not always to be bought in the shops. Mum walked all over to get food for us so queuing became part of living. Fish and chip shops sold chips and battered collops instead of fish which was in short supply. Sometimes if you were lucky you got a sausagemeat cake instead of a fish cake. There was no fresh fruit available in the shops, bananas, oranges and grapefruit could not be imported because space was needed on the ships for grain to make bread. We put up with this because we believed we were in the front line, next to our troops in this war against evil and an evil man named Hitler. Houses were bombed in Bradford, as too was the station at Laisterdyke where I had caught the train to Pudsey and Stanningley. When it was moonlight we sort of expected that the air raid sirens would go off and soon get used to having a broken night's sleep. At Cutler Place we had gone down into the cellar, but at Beverley Street we did not have one so we just got up out of bed, went into the living room and crawled under the large square table there.

Every news bulletin over the wireless was listened to intently, the loss of men and ships greeted with tears and sorrow. At this time we did not have very much to rejoice about as we seemed to be losing out all the time.

A very dear friend of mine had been called up straight away as he was in the Territorials. A lovely young man called Edward Lister, who was the youngest of the family and lived with his parents at a grocery and off-licence shop down at the bottom of Mount Street. They were really quite well off in those days and Eddy, as we called him, was a nice looking, cheerful lad who always had a smile on his face and was very good natured. We often went to the pictures together but were in no way serious about it. On going overseas with the BEF, Eddy wrote to me saying he was an Army lorry driver taking men and equipment to different places. Sometimes in the letters he would forget and write down some place in Belgium where he had been but this was always blacked out (censored) before I received the letter. We wrote about once a week to each other. I told him about things over here, where I had been, what I had been doing and news of his friends back home. In one letter he asked me to have a photograph taken so I could send it on to him. Lots of the men had pictures of wives and girlfriends to show but he did not have one. I went down to 'Jerome's' on Tyrell Street at that time, near 'Collinson's Cafe'. I had three, head and shoulders, sepia pictures taken which came out quite good so I sent one to Eddy with the inscription 'To Eddy with love, Vera'. He wrote back to thank me for it and said his pals had kidded him on about keeping quiet about his girl friend.

It was a terrible time of anxiety for all who had loved ones in the Army at that time when all our troops were evacuated from Dunkirk. I had not heard from Edward for about ten days and I hoped he had got safely away. One evening about two weeks later we were sat in the living room when there was a knock at the front door so I went to see who it was. An elderly lady stood there and as soon as I saw her face I knew it was Edward's mother she looked so like him. I asked her in after she said she was looking for a Miss Vera Magson. Dad and the boys were out at the time which was very fortunate. We asked Mrs Lister to sit on the settee. She sat there with a small bundle of letters in her hand, tears rolling down her face as she told us Eddy had been killed at Dunkirk. A letter from his Commanding Officer said he had been driving a lorry full of men down one of the lanes leading to the beach where our ships were waiting to transport them back home. Some German planes, mostly fighter planes and some with bombs as well, were flying over the lorries full of troops firing machine guns at them. Edward was shot as he was driving the men in his lorry and died right away. She had brought my

"… he asked me to have a photograph taken …"   *Photo: Author's collection*

121

letters and photo back, she showed me his wallet where he had kept them and also the watch his Mum and Dad had bought him for his 21st birthday. I could not express my feelings to her, I was too shattered. She had wanted to meet me as my photo and letters were the only ones he had kept. I told her we had been very good friends and that was all, we had not been courting or going out 'seriously', though I knew that perhaps he had liked me a bit more than just a good friend.

When I think about the war now, it is not the great battles that we won or lost, the ships that were sunk, the planes we lost in the air battles, the defeat of the Germans and Japs – no, in my memory of that time is an elderly lady sat on our settee, clutching a few torn letters in an old wallet, tears streaming down her face and sobbing her heart out as she told us about her beloved son – that's what war is all about to me.

Shortly after this I made up my mind that I was going to do more for my war effort than sat burling and mending. So one Monday morning instead of going to work I went into town to the Labour Exchange. I had an interview with a lady and told her I wanted to go on munitions. She asked me if I would be willing to go away from home but I explained that I was still needed at home so I wanted to work on munitions somewhere near enough for me to get home each night. She told me that they had just started a training school for women at 'Croft's Engineers' at Thornbury. This was a long established firm that made gear boxes and had their own foundry. I was very interested in Croft's, as it was only about 15 minutes walk from home. She made out a form for me to sign and gave me a card to take up to Croft's, then she asked me where I was working at present. When I told her I was in textiles at Priestley's she said I would not be able to leave there without written permission from the manager as they too were doing war work. This did put a spanner in the works as far as I was concerned. The thought of going to ask Claude for his consent really went against the grain, as the saying goes. However, on thinking it over I knew that if I was to get away from there this was the only way. I went into work after lunch and asked Annie if she could arrange for me to see Claude. At about 3.00 in the afternoon a message came through that he would see me in his office. When I went in I knew I was going to have a real battle on my hands. There had never been much love lost between us from the time I had told him I would not stop singing in the workroom. He listened to my request for release to go work at Croft's. When I had finished he told me he would think it over and that was all for now. So I came out of the office no wiser.

The week seemed to crawl along, each day I hoped he would come in and tell me his decision. The women I worked with all understood how I felt, and although they would miss me and the songs I sang for them, they understood me wanting to do more for the war effort. It got to Friday afternoon, the wages came round but still no word from Claude. I think I got to the stage where I felt sure he meant to keep me there. At about 4.30 he came into the mending room, came up to me, put down my 'cards' and the form signed by him releasing me from Priestley's. I thanked him but he just ignored me and walked out. When the door shut behind him we all gave a little cheer and I was wished luck in my new job. As at Leigh Mills I had no regrets about leaving and so my days in textiles came to an end. I had earned some good money, better than in an office but the conditions in two of the three firms were those of the Victorian era. Speight's had been different altogether, a lovely modern mill, nice surroundings with good working conditions. After the war I went back to work at Speight's for quite a few years. Berta was still there and we even had a wireless to listen to 'Housewives' Choice' and 'Music while you work'. I spent about five years there after the war and very happy I was, but that's another story.

A couple of weeks after starting at Croft's, my boyfriend Sam was called up into the Air Force. He had been going to night classes at Charlton Street Grammar School for a navigation course in algebra and mathematics as he wanted to be in air-crew. Everything seemed to be happening at once for me. A new job and him going in the Forces. Before he left we got engaged. The ring was bought from 'Hardy's', a well known jewellers in Bradford at that time, which was at the bottom of Leeds Road which in those days ran right down and round to nearly the front of the Town Hall. I chose a twin crossover diamond ring, claw set with the shoulders set in platinum and chip diamonds. The cost was £12.10s, a huge amount in those days. I was so proud of my ring but could only wear it at weekends as the work I did at Croft's was so dirty.

Sam went off in the Air Force and I settled down to war work. The hours were longer than in textiles, 7.30 to 12.00, 12.45 to 5.15 and then overtime until 7.30 at night. We had to do three nights of overtime each week and we also had to work Saturday mornings. All the women wore boiler suits. I had never worn trousers before in my life but soon got used to the freedom they afforded. I was put to work on a drilling and tapping machine that involved drilling holes in the iron casings and then tapping the rings round the inside of the hole for the screws to fit

Marriage to Sam, 1942.   *Photo: Author's collection*

in. I liked the work very much, but the standing on my feet for long hours each day killed me for a few weeks until I got used to it. You see I had been used to sitting all day when I was mending. The work was very dirty as all the machines used a great deal of oil and also the bits that came out whilst drilling made your hands dirty, but I felt I was doing my bit for the war. We were on a standard rate of pay but only being eighteen years old I did not get the full pay, but with the overtime I put in I made about as much as an average week in the mill. As I got more used to the job and could do it without supervision I realised that the men were earning twice as much as me for doing the same amount of work. This was a bone of contention with all the women who worked there. We all felt it unfair that because we were women we we were paid less than the men for doing the same amount of work. That was in the days before equality and the Sex Discrimination Act so we just moaned about it but got on with the job.

Even then I had not got away from the burling and mending. There was a small textile mill up Parsonage Road, Turnpenny's I think it was called, they were doing cloth for the Army and were wanting burlers to burl pieces at home as they had no more vacant tables in the mill. Mother saw the manager and told him I was a fully experienced burler and mender so he agreed to send her three pieces a week if I would show her how to burl them. Mum was thrilled at the prospect of getting a pound or two for herself, so I had to spend three nights a week for about a month showing her how to do burling. She did the work on the top of the large square dining table we had in the living room. So every night, straight after tea all was cleared away and Mum and I struggled with a large khaki piece over the table. I showed her how to use the burling irons and scissors and how to lift the knot to undo it and how to draw thick ends and thin them, there was no mending to do. So on the evenings I was not working over at Croft's I was helping Mum or writing to Sam.

Winter was a hard time for everyone as fuel was hard to come by. Everyone had coal fires, there was no gas central heating or electric in those days for working class people. Fuel was needed for the war effort so we had to make do with what we could get. I remember seeing people going to the Gas Works down Birkshall Lane with old prams or pushchairs, or anything on wheels, to enable them to get bags of coke that were sold cheap to mix with the coal to put on the fires. Also there was a man who came round with a coal cart who sold coal bricks. These were square blocks of compressed coal dust made into 'bricks' with water, these along with one or two pieces of coal helped to keep the fire going. Another trouble was the clothing coupons. You were only allowed so many per person and as children were always growing out of shoes and clothes this was a real problem. Everything you could lay your hands on was made into clothes – old curtains, blanket; used parachutes were good for under clothes, if you could get one. Everything was recycled and used again, we all looked alike, drab, dreary, shabby people but as everyone was the same, except for those with money to buy goods on the 'black market', we just got on with it. People who had money did not go without either food or clothes. The old sayings 'money buys anything' or 'money talks' was certainly true in those days. The ordinary people in our part of the country did without, put up with shortages and raids and the blackouts but they just went on living as best they could.

I shall never forget those war years; blackouts over the windows, not enough food or clothes, the raids when the planes came over, the nights when the sirens sounded and we were kept awake half the night, but had still to get up the next day to put in a full days work. Our only enjoyment was the picture houses where we all went to see the Hollywood films that lent a bit of colour to our hard working lives. The colour films were lovely to see with the beautiful dresses the stars wore. We saw films like 'Hello Frisco, Hello' with Alice Faye, 'Waterloo Bridge' with Viv Leigh, 'Gone with the Wind', 'Rebecca', 'Hollywood Canteen' and all the Betty Grable movies. These kept us going and brought a bit of colour and glamour into our lives.

If you could afford a meal out, Collinson's Cafe was a very popular place. The meals they managed to put on were nothing short of a miracle! They were always nicely served and there was a trio of musicians playing modern and classical music on the platform on the upper floor. You could go in for just tea and toast in those days, and it made a welcome change from meals at home. It was the one thing I did treat myself to on a Saturday afternoon – tea at Collinson's or the New Victoria Cafe, and then on to a good film after or to a dance at the New Vic or The Queen's or the King's which were the Windsor Baths.

Sam had one or two leaves during this time and we had talked about getting married before he went overseas. His opinion was that if we got married I would get an allowance from him which could be saved up as a little nest egg for us to start with after the war. I could see the sense in this, as I would still be at home with Mum and Dad but would be able to save quite a bit. So I began collecting a few clothing coupons for my wedding dress. We were going to be married at Greenhill Methodist Church as my chapel at Cutler Heights was not licensed for weddings. I had my dress made at a dressmakers up Wakefield Road, she also made my three bridesmaids' dresses which were pale blue silk. Our families knew we were going to get married if Sam had to go overseas so everyone did their best to get organised. We could not make definite plans as we had no idea when the embarkation leave would come but Sam had told me they were getting fitted out with tropical kit so thought he would be going to the Middle East or India. They never told them where they were going as it was a matter of national security so all destinations were purely guesswork.

I for my part had arranged all things at this end, we were going to have the reception at Cutler Heights and cater for ourselves. Neighbours and relations had given tins of things and we had been lucky enough to get a wedding cake made, all iced ready for the day. I had a brown suit made for going away, a turquoise blouse with a tie neck and a brown 'Deanna Durbin' hat with a large brim and big turquoise feather up the back. We were going away to Morecambe for a few days – so everything was ready. In February 1943 I got a telegram from Sam saying 'I am coming home on the 25th February and will get a special licence if you will marry me, Love Sam'. I sent a short telegram back saying 'Everything is ready including me, Love Vera'. So we were married at Greenhill Methodist Church by the Reverend Alexander Park Gilbertson at 2.00 on 27th February 1943 which was a lovely, bright cold day when the sun shone on us both.

So on that day I started my new life as the wife of an Air Force Corporal home on embarkation leave – but that's another story!

My Family Today (1986). Left to right: Brother Donald with Betty, Les, my husband, and me (and Suzi), brother Basil (with Doreen).